The Remarkable Adventures of
"Portuguese Joe" Silvey

JEAN BARMAN

A RAINCOAST MONOGRAPH

H A R B O U R   P U B L I S H I N G

Published by
Harbour Publishing Co. Ltd.
P.O. Box 219, Madeira Park, BC V0N 2H0
www.harbourpublishing.com

04 05 06 07 08 09 7 6 5 4 3 2

Edited by Mary Schendlinger
Cover and page design by Martin Nichols
Maps by Gary McManus
Cover image of Portuguese Joe from City of Vancouver Archives, Port P656;
photo of schooner from BC Archives, H-02689; back cover photo courtesy Jessica Casey
Printed and bound in Canada

Harbour Publishing acknowledges financial support from the Government of Canada through the Book Publishing Industry Development Program and the Canada Council for the Arts, and from the Province of British Columbia through the British Columbia Arts Council and the Book Publisher's Tax Credit through the Ministry of Provincial Revenue.

THE CANADA COUNCIL | LE CONSEIL DES ARTS
FOR THE ARTS | DU CANADA
SINCE 1957 | DEPUIS 1957

BRITISH
COLUMBIA
ARTS COUNCIL
Supported by the Province of British Columbia

National Library of Canada Cataloguing in Publication
Barman, Jean, 1939–
    The remarkable adventures of Portuguese Joe Silvey / Jean Barman.

Includes index.
    ISBN 1-55017-326-X

    1. Silvey, Joe, 1828-1902. 2. Portuguese Canadians—British Columbia—Biography. 3. Pioneers—British Columbia—Biography. 4. British Columbia—Biography. I. Title.
FC3823.1.S54B37 2004   971.1'03'092   C2004-900912-5

Dedicated to Portuguese Joe's great-great-great-grandsons Kyle and Cole Silvey for asking me to tell the story, and to Portuguese Joe and his family for making the story possible in the first place:

Joseph Silvey, 1828–1902

Khaltinaht/Mary Ann, c. 1845–c. 1872

Kwahama Kwatleematt/Lucy, c. 1857–1934

Elizabeth, c. 1867–1945

Josephine, c. 1872–1930

Domingo, 1874–1941

Mary, 1877–1941

Joseph, 1879–1940

John, 1882–1907

Tony, 1884–1967

Manuel, 1886–1916

Clara, 1889–1893

Andrew Henry, 1890–1966

Lena, 1895–1957

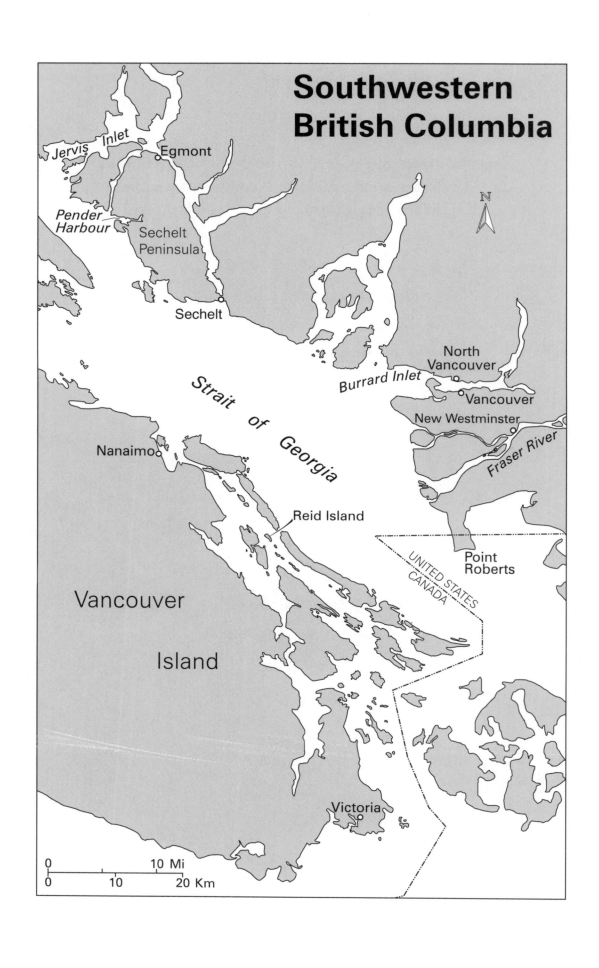

Southwestern British Columbia

Jervis Inlet

Egmont

Pender Harbour

Sechelt Peninsula

Sechelt

North Vancouver

Burrard Inlet

Vancouver

New Westminster

Fraser River

Strait of Georgia

Nanaimo

Reid Island

Vancouver

Island

UNITED STATES

CANADA

Point Roberts

Victoria

0   10 Mi

0   10   20 Km

Contents

Preface

There is a Portuguese saying that God is everywhere, but the Portuguese were there first. Accordingly, it should come as no surprise that Portuguese Joe Silvey was one of the earliest pioneers of what is now British Columbia. Joe Silvey was only one of many Portuguese who reached both the east and west coasts of Canada long before 1867, the year of Confederation (British Columbia joined in 1871). In fact, 2004 is the 300th anniversary of Canada's first letter carrier, Pedro da Silva of New France, an occasion that has been honoured with the issue of a commemorative stamp by Canada Post.

Portuguese Joe Silvey sought his fortune in the gold rush of 1858 at a time when the non-aboriginal population of British Columbia exploded from about 1,000 to 20,000 or more in a matter of months. Victoria, a sleepy town of about 400 people, became a sprawling tent city overnight, filled with gold seekers from every corner of the world.

Although Joe was unlucky in his search for gold, he did find a beautiful wife in the unspoiled paradise that would become Vancouver. His wedding to Khaltinaht, the granddaughter of the legendary Chief Kiapilano, took place at Musqueam, and the newlyweds set off in a canoe piled high with blankets to their first home at Point Roberts. Later Joe opened a saloon at the corner of Abbott and Water streets, across the street from Gregorio Fernandez's general store. He lived at Brockton Point, in what later became Stanley Park, with other pioneers: the legendary whaler Portuguese Pete (Peter Smith); Joe Gonsalves, aka Portuguese Joe No. 3; and Vancouver's first police officer, Tomkins Brew. All of them—except Fernandez, who remained a bachelor—married aboriginal women.

After the tragic death of his wife Khaltinaht, Joe Silvey found yet another beautiful wife, Kwahama Kwatleematt (Lucy) from Sechelt, and together they raised 11 children on Reid Island off the northwest tip of Galiano Island. Joe worked hard to raise his family and protect them from the prejudices of the times. He fished for dogfish and herring, which he sold to loggers and visiting ships, he built boats and houses, he planted orchards, he operated a store and he entertained his family with his mandolin and Portuguese dances. He never returned to his homeland, the island of Pico in the Azores, aka the Westerly Isles—Portuguese islands in the middle of the Atlantic Ocean, more than 1,000 miles off the coast of Portugal on the same latitude as New York City.

Like his countrymen from the Azores, Madeira and Cape Verde islands, Joe established deep roots in British Columbia. These men, like other pioneers from every corner of the world, contributed to the building of BC. Joe practically founded the fishing industry and obtained the first herring seine licence in the province. His Brockton Point neighbour, the legendary Portuguese Pete, started the whaling industry; Joe Gonsalves of Madeira built the first deep-sea docks on the Sunshine Coast with the help of the "black" Azorean, Joe Perry; John Silva of Cape Verde, later of Gabriola Island, planted what may have been the province's first apple orchard on Mayne Island; John Enos (Ignacio) of the island of Santa Maria in the Azores, the first European settler at Nanoose Bay, helped build the bridges of Nanaimo. In Victoria, Joseph Morais owned and operated a hotel, restaurant and miners' exchange in 1861. The Bittancourt and Norton brothers, from Sao Miguel and Flores islands (Azores), respectively, developed dairies, coal mines and quarries on Salt Spring Island.

Now, for the first time, the respected historian and professor Jean Barman gives us a very human glimpse of the life of one of these pioneer builders of British Columbia, Portuguese Joe Silvey. She traces his adventures, his fortunes and misfortunes through the stories told by his children and their descendants. In this very personal, heartwarming monograph, she brings one family to life, thereby providing us with a better understanding of the untold lives of hundreds of other early pioneers whose contributions and sacrifices made British Columbia what it is today.

—Manuel A. Azevedo
Vancouver

Introduction

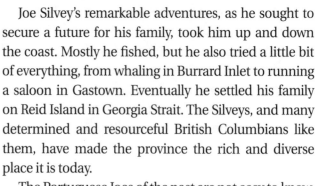

Portuguese Joe Silvey was born in the Azores, a Portuguese possession in the middle of the Atlantic Ocean. In the 1850s he came to British Columbia and decided to stay. At that time the gold rush attracted many thousands of men hoping to get rich quick. Most of them left in disgust almost as soon as they came, but not Joe. He fell in love with Khaltinaht, a Musqueam and Squamish woman, but she died just as they were starting their family. Joe then married a Sechelt woman named Kwahama, with whom he raised 10 children to adulthood.

An illiterate whaler from the Azores, Portuguese Joe was an enterprising businessman whose adventures as a saloon-keeper, fisherman, whaler and shop owner earned him friends up and down the southern BC coast. City of Vancouver Archives, Port P656

Joe Silvey's remarkable adventures, as he sought to secure a future for his family, took him up and down the coast. Mostly he fished, but he also tried a little bit of everything, from whaling in Burrard Inlet to running a saloon in Gastown. Eventually he settled his family on Reid Island in Georgia Strait. The Silveys, and many determined and resourceful British Columbians like them, have made the province the rich and diverse place it is today.

The Portuguese Joes of the past are not easy to know. Most of us remember our grandparents, or at least something about them: we can picture them in our minds and we may have tucked away some letters they wrote. We are far less likely to know much about our grandparents' grandparents. They may have been illiterate, as Joseph Silvey was, or found reading and writing uncomfortable. Their lives survive mainly as stories that have passed down through the generations.

Family stories are about belonging. Each one is unique, but all of them are also parts of larger stories. Portuguese Joe has hundreds of descendants across British Columbia and beyond, each of whom is fortunate enough to have "genes" or inherited characteristics that come from him. He is part of them every day of their lives, and so are the stories that have been passed down to them. It is through the stories they have to tell, and are willing to share with others, that we can glimpse Portuguese Joe's extraordinary adventures. By doing so, we come to understand a bit better who we are as British Columbians and Canadians.

In the Azores

For as long as he could remember, young Joseph Silvey had heard stories about places far away from his island home in the middle of the Atlantic Ocean. Joe lived on Pico, one of nine islands that together are known as the Azores.

More than 400 years before Joe was born, ships from Portugal landed on the Azores and the islands were claimed for Portugal. The men and women who settled in the Azores made their living mostly by farming and fishing. They brought their way of life from the "mainland," as Portugal came to be known. All of them adhered to the precepts of the Catholic Church, and they took large families for granted. Men were responsible for supporting their wives and children with their labour, while women held sway in the home. Women were to respect their menfolk, and children their parents and all others older than themselves. Azoreans maintained such a traditional peasant lifestyle despite growing contact with outsiders, mainly explorers and merchants of many different countries who sailed between Europe and North America and stopped over in the Azores to get supplies. The stories these visitors told about the places whence they came and where they were heading were part of the folklore of Joe's childhood.

It was not easy for Joe's parents to make a living for their family. Pico Island is just 42 kilometres long and 15 kilometres wide, and has at its centre a huge volcano (Pico means "point" in Portuguese). The volcano, known as Pico Alto, or "high peak," towers 2,330 metres above the water. The only arable land on the island is a small rocky strip along the shore, at the foot of Pico Alto. Long before Joe was born, Pico Islanders gathered the loose stones and made fences to mark out the boundaries between their

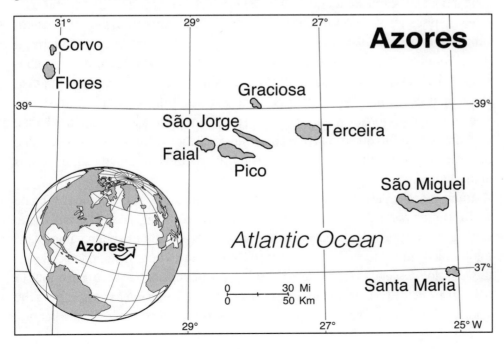

In the late 1830s, Pico Islanders began hunting the whales that migrated past their island. © Copyright New Bedford Whaling Museum

hard-worked plots. Most families grew potatoes as a subsistence crop, ensuring that they would have something to eat during the winter. Some pastured cattle on the slopes of the volcano. Lower down, others grew figs to be sold or grapes for wine, but many more depended on the sea.

Pico Island families had fished for generations. When Joe was a child in the 1830s, they were also hunting whales, which migrated past the island. The animals were caught not for their meat but for their blubber, which was boiled for its valuable oil.

Ships in search of whales had begun to arrive in the Azores from the northeastern United States years earlier, when Joe's father was a boy. World whaling was dominated by the Americans, who had their principal home port at New Bedford, Massachusetts, about 80 kilometres south of Boston. The ships stopped to pick up supplies at Horta on nearby Faial Island, and took on crew as needed. Men wanting jobs came from all over the Azores, especially from the poorly endowed Pico Island. Joe's father, or perhaps it was his uncle, told him about sailing all the way to North America in the *Morning Star*, a ship that regularly hired young men from Pico and the other islands of the Azores.

Young Joe Silvey also heard stories about a Scottish grandfather. In one version he was a seaman named Simmons who owned his own ship and sailed wherever in the world profit was to be had. Indeed, records show that a whaling captain named Simmons sailed out of Massachusetts during the mid-19th century. In another version of the story, Joe descended from one of the soldiers sent by Britain to Portugal in 1808 to help drive out the French after they invaded during the Napoleonic wars. Some of the soldiers liked Portugal so much they settled there or in the Azores after the fighting was over. Joe once told his daughter that his mother's, or possibly his father's, Scottish ancestry was the reason why he was lighter-complexioned than most Portuguese. Elizabeth remembered her father as being "fair haired, with rosy cheeks." According to another descendant, "When Silvey men grow a beard, it's red." In family lore, Portuguese Joe has blue eyes and his son Henry has "greeny blue" ones. This inheritance may explain why Joe used the name Joseph Silvia Seamens when taking up land in British Columbia.

Going to Sea

Joe Silvey was 12 years old when he began to have his own adventures. His father decided the time had come for Joe and his older brother João, or John, to learn to make a living, and the next time he went whaling, he took the boys with him. Joe left Pico Island and his mother behind forever. They likely never even wrote to each other. Joe had not gone to school and never learned to read and write. These activities were not considered necessary in a society where the land and the water gave people a livelihood. For Joe, the sea provided a means of survival time and time again.

Young Joe soon found out that whaling was no easy job. A typical ship's crew consisted of 25 to 30 men: the shipmaster and his mates; a cook; artisans including a carpenter, cooper and blacksmith; several boatsteers; and seamen. Many of the recruits taken on in the Azores worked as boatsteers. They were the men responsible for navigating the small double-ended open whaleboats, about eight metres long, from which whales were harpooned.

Once whales were sighted—"there she blows!"—the ship manoeuvred to within a kilometre or two of the pod and the men launched the three or four whaleboats, which were slung on the sides of the ship. Each boat had five oarsmen, one of whom was the boatsteer. Once one of the boats got close enough, its boatsteer harpooned the whale. The harpoon was attached to the whaleboat by a line, which was played out as the hooked animal thrashed about in the water. The oars were brought into

Countless men from Pico left behind their island to better their prospects aboard American whaling ships that stopped in the Azores to pick up supplies. © Copyright New Bedford Whaling Museum

Whaling was a dangerous business, especially for the boatsteers, who were responsible for navigating the small double-ended whaleboats and harpooning the giant animals.
© Copyright New Bedford Whaling Museum

the whaleboat and the boatsteer took charge as the boat was pulled through the water behind the whale, sometimes for hours on end. When the hooked whale grew tired enough that it could be approached by the whaleboat, the men stabbed the animal to death with spears or lances. The harpoon was then reeled in, and the line was used to tow the carcass to the ship.

Killing the whale was only the first step. Now the crew had to boil the carcass in order to release the oil from the blubber just beneath the skin. The carcass was tied up on the side of the ship and the blubber was stripped off, cut in pieces and melted in huge iron cauldrons. This was hazardous work that required several days of intense labour by all aboard. As soon as more whales were sighted, the process began all over again.

Capturing whales was dangerous, so perhaps it is not surprising that Joe's father died of heart trouble while on board ship. According to the story Joe told his children, his father called his two sons to come to his side. He "was sitting in a big chair, and he told the boys to be good boys when they grew up, and then he just sunk down in the chair and was dead, while they were with him." Shortly thereafter, Joe's brother drowned.

Joe Silvey was left all alone in a tough occupation in which men were sometimes valued less for their hard work than for their willingness to endure poor working conditions and low wages. Azoreans were seen as men who would put up with such hardships. Two-thirds of the ship's profits went to the businessmen who had furnished the money for the trip, and one-third went to the workers on board. Each man received a predetermined portion of the net profit. Workers were only paid at the end of a voyage, which might last two or three years or even longer. By the 1840s, the average crew member's cut was considerably less than what he could earn in a Massachusetts factory. Whaling entrepreneurs believed that foreigners, particularly those who were illiterate and unskilled, as were most young Azoreans, were less likely to desert when another opportunity beckoned at some port of call.

Such prejudice made men like Joe restless. The whaling historian Elmo Hohman has described how, during the years when Joe was young, "more and more the intelligent and ambitious young American refused to go to sea, ... least of all on a whaler." According to Hohman, "as the better types of Americans forsook the forecastles, their bunks were filled by criminal or lascivious adventurers, by a motley collection of South Sea Islanders known as Kanakas, by cross-breed negroes and Portuguese from the Azores and the Cape Verdes, and by the outcasts and renegades from all the merchant services of both the Old World and the New." He blamed the decline of whaling on the "ignorance, incompetence, and general inefficiency" of such men. In fact, the decline resulted from the discovery in 1859 in Pennsylvania of ground oil, which was a good substitute for whale oil and much more economical to harvest and process.

No wonder many recruits from the Azores and elsewhere who manned the hundreds of whaling vessels roaming the world's oceans each year began to seek other employment. Young men like Joe Silvey did not think of going home: Pico Island was unable to provide a good living for all of its population, and crop failures made conditions even worse during the mid-19th century. The island's main food crop was hit by potato blight, and a grape disease severely reduced wine production. Joe did not have much incentive to return home.

Whaling was not a good living, but it did offer opportunities to begin anew. When an American vessel returned to its home port, usually in Massachusetts, the employees were paid off and discharged. Members of Joe's family, including a sister, are said to have settled there. As well, some crew members jumped ship. By the time gold was discovered in 1849 in California, ships were travelling long distances in search of whales and men were dropping off without permission in ever greater numbers. On the way to whaling grounds in the Arctic waters of the Pacific Ocean, ships stopped for supplies at San Francisco and other west coast ports, and men slipped away—so many of them, both officers and crew, that the practice became almost commonplace.

Joe was one of these men. He decided the time had come to explore the opportunities these faraway places might hold. By now he knew some English and was confident about fending for himself in a strange land. On one of his trips, as the story has come down through Joe's family, the ship on which he was working got in a serious accident off the Pacific coast and had to put into port to make repairs. Joe and five other crew members, all Portuguese, seized the opportunity to slip away.

Once a whale was killed, its carcass was lashed to the side of the ship and its blubber stripped off for processing.
© Copyright New Bedford Whaling Museum

British Columbia-Bound

Just as it is not possible to know Joe Silvey's precise name or his birth year, we cannot know how or when he got to British Columbia. What repeats itself time and time again in the stories that have passed down through the generations is that he "jumped ship" with "five other Portuguese men" and did so from "a whaler." In one version of the story he landed in 1849 in California; in another, in 1852 at the fur-trade post of Fort Victoria in the British colony of Vancouver Island. In the 1901 census Joe Silvey gave the date as 1860, which seems most plausible: not only did it come from him, but in all versions of the story, Joe and his fellow deserters began searching for gold almost immediately. They might have done so first in California, where a gold rush was in full force from 1848. It is more likely they headed up the Fraser River to take advantage of the gold rush that began there in 1858 and gradually moved north to the Cariboo. As to the location at which the men slipped away, it might have been Victoria, but it might also have been, as one story suggests, Point Roberts, a tip of land on the British Columbia mainland that lies within the boundaries of the United States.

Wherever the Portuguese men came ashore, it is very likely that the first news they heard was about the fabulous riches to be had from gold. Perhaps they deserted because they had already heard the news. Ever since gold was discovered in California, stories had spread about how easy it was to get rich quick. In the spring of 1858, news got out about discoveries on the Fraser River. Later that year the mainland became a separate British colony named British Columbia. Men came from California and from all over the world in search of their fortunes. Now, very likely, Joe and his friends were among them.

In one version of the stories in Joe Silvey's family, the Portuguese newcomers got a hold of a dugout canoe and headed up the Fraser River. They paddled past the rough mainland capital of New Westminster, past the long-time fur-trading post of Fort Langley, and on they went. They might have gotten as far as Yale at the entrance to the Fraser Canyon. Perhaps they were already gold mining when they were warned about the local Natives. The Indians, they were told, wanted to get rid of newcomers, whom they considered to be trespassing on their land. The young Portuguese men became convinced that they were about to be attacked, and they did not want to be killed. So

In one version of Portuguese Joe's story, he jumped ship with five other men at Point Roberts, acquired a dugout canoe and paddled up the Fraser River to join the gold rush. Later, he returned here with his bride.
BC Archives PDP02617

they took their canoe back down river as fast as they could, back to where they had jumped ship.

When the men were almost back at Point Roberts, as one story goes, some Musqueam Indians appeared on the bank of the Fraser River. Joe and the others were convinced that their time had come: they would not be able to escape twice with their lives. Then they realized the Indians were not hostile. Indeed, they were beckoning the newcomers toward them. Grand Chief Kiapilano of the Squamish Indians, who lived farther north on the north shore of Burrard Inlet, was visiting his mother's people at Musqueam. He stood in the middle of the crowd to welcome the men ashore. They were tired and in desperate need of something to eat, and they decided to take a chance. Much to their relief, the Indians treated them kindly, gave them food and invited them to stay the night.

The next morning, as the men continued on in their canoe across the Georgia Strait to the gold-rush boomtown of Victoria, Joe kept thinking about the friendship extended by the Musqueam people. After he had earned a bit of money and gotten some supplies together, he returned to Point Roberts. He built himself a cabin and opened a little store for passing miners such as he himself had been, not so long before. Intent on becoming self-sufficient, Joe also farmed, fished and hunted.

Compared with the austere living conditions of Pico Island, Point Roberts must have seemed a paradise.

It may have been at about this point in time that Joe Silvey began to be known as "Portuguese Joe." Perhaps it was his accent but it was also very likely his pride in his ethnic origins. Throughout his life, Joe remained very proud of being Portuguese.

Finding a Wife

Joe Silvey settled in Point Roberts and found himself a wife. In fact, that may have been his reason for returning. The granddaughter of Chief Kiapilano and of his wife Homulchesun from Musqueam had caught Joe's eye. Khaltinaht was the child of Kiapilano's son Kwileetrock and a woman named Sukwaht, whose brother Sam Kwee-ahkult was chief at the Squamish village of Whoi Whoi on the south shore of Burrard Inlet in what would become Stanley Park. Khaltinaht lived at Musqueam with her grandmother's people. Joe later told his eldest daughter that "she was a pretty girl with dark eyes, and hair down to her middle; large deep soft eyes." He soon discovered that she felt as kindly toward him as he did toward her.

Joe's eldest daughter Elizabeth shared her father's story about how he asked his prospective grandfather-in-law for Khaltinaht's hand in marriage. "Mother and Father were out in a canoe, and then afterwards Father said by signs, to the old chief, Chief Kiapilano, that he wanted my mother for his wife, and could he have her; all by signs. Then the old chief said, by signs, that he could; waved his hand and arm with a motion signifying to 'take her.' He motioned with his right arm and waved, quickly, upward and outward."

In a landscape dominated by thick vegetation and towering trees, Europeans like Portuguese Joe Silvey quickly adopted the canoe as a means of transportation. For Joe, a canoe ride with the lovely Khaltinaht sparked the romance that led to their marriage. Vancouver Public Library Special Collections VPL 12706

The marriage ceremony respected aboriginal practice. "In those days they were married under Indian law…The old Chief, Chief Kiapilano, took my father, and the chief of the Musqueams took my mother, and the two chiefs put them together…They had canoes and canoes and canoes, all drawn up on the beach, and a great crowd of Indians, and they had a great time. They had a lot of stuff for the festivities, Indian blankets and all sorts of things, and threw it all away; they had a great big potlatch. And, then, they put my mother and father in a great big canoe with a lot of blankets, made them sit on top of the blankets, and then brought them over to home at Point Roberts."

Joe Silvey and Khaltinaht may have been the young couple that a passing gold miner encountered at "Point Roberts, just within the boundary line of American territory," in the fall of 1862. It was commonplace for men of Portuguese descent to be called "Portuguese Joe." There were several such men around Burrard Inlet, so it's impossible to know for sure whether or not this was our Joe Silvey. "Here we met a retired sailor named Portugee Joe, who had gone in for a comfortable existence upon a very small farm, supplemented by the proceeds of his gun and fishing-boat. Joe had taken unto himself a maid of the forest, and had built himself a large snug log-house…There was plenty of room for all of us, whiskey galore, and any amount of

Portuguese Joe and Khaltinaht settled in Burrard Inlet, where he fished for dogfish to support them and she was close to members of her Musqueam and Squamish families. BC Archives A-00978

game and fish to be had for the killing...We had milk and butter too, for Joe managed to keep a couple of cows on his little paddock." The men undertook various hunting adventures together over the next two weeks. "One part of the elk we kept for Joe's household, and his wife set to work to cure the hams."

Going Fishing

Joe wanted more than just a bare living. It was time for another adventure.

More and more newcomers were settling around Victoria and New Westminster. A lumber mill began operating on the north shore of Burrard Inlet in 1863, bringing new opportunities. Not only did settlers have to eat, sawmills needed oil to keep in good condition the saws and other machinery used to cut lumber into wood. Joe thought back to the means of earning a living his father had taught him in the faraway Azores, and he knew exactly how to get both oil and food from the sea. Portuguese Joe went fishing.

On March 4, 1866, a strong tide forced a schooner heading north in Georgia Strait to anchor in Active Pass between Mayne and Galiano islands. There the crew encountered "some Fisher men," one of whom "generally known by the generic name of 'Portugee Joe' visited us." A long conversation ensued, which one of the men on board described in some detail. "Joe had just caught lb 500 of fish—enough for the Westminster & Victoria markets—he sent them up by the [boat] 'Enterprise.' He caught them with double hooked lines but the Dog fish (*anarchias suckleyi*) were very troublesome to him, biting off the hooks." A relative of sturgeon, dogfish were caught not for food but for their oil.

A natural salesman, Portuguese Joe sold dogfish oil to companies such as the Moodyville sawmill, on the north shore of Burrard Inlet, as lubricant for their machinery and skid trails. City of Vancouver Archives, Mi P43

"Portugee Joe," as his name was pronounced by those who knew him, retailed his adventures of the past year. "He told me at first that he had lost $150 by his salmon fishing & on enquiry found that if he had kept them three weeks longer he might have made that sum in addition—a rather amusing way of putting it!" Joe was becoming an astute businessman. "Joe made by his own Confession last summer by salting & smoking salmon more than $2,000. He had caught a shark from the liver of which he had extracted 20 gals of oil."

Settling Down

By 1866 the gold excitement was over. To save money, the two British colonies of Vancouver Island and British Columbia were amalgamated into a single colony named British Columbia. It was men like Joe Silvey, able to do work other than mining, who decided to stay. Portuguese Joe's new life offered him more than he could have found back in the Azores. His success with fishing gave him confidence about what he could achieve with the help of Khaltinaht, who by now also went by the English name of Mary Ann.

Portuguese Joe began to think of settling down. On March 23, 1867, the *British Colonist*, a Victoria newspaper, reported: "Joseph Silva, a native of Portugal, took the oaths…and became a naturalized British subject." According to the story passed down to his grandson, he "was the first Portuguese in Canada to receive British citizenship and was called 'Portugee Joe No. 1' for that reason." It seems likely that this man was indeed our Portuguese Joe. What the declaration meant was that he could now vote and exercise the civil rights available to all other British subjects in this British colony of British Columbia. Very importantly, he could acquire land. Indeed, on the very same

Joe Silvey's resolve to remain in British Columbia became clear the day he chose to become a British subject. His naturalization was reported in *The Colonist*, on March 23, 1867.
BC Archives

Having grown up on an island where land was limited, Portuguese Joe quickly saw the advantages of living in a scarcely populated corner of the world where he could acquire property for little or no money. At left is his request for land at Mary Ann Point, Galiano Island.
BC Archives GR766

day, "Joseph Silva" signed with his *X* a request to preempt 100 acres at "Maryanns Point—Galiano Isl[an]d." Joe named the land—located off Active Pass, where he had anchored a year earlier—after his wife.

One of the reasons Portuguese Joe became proprietorial was his upcoming, or recent, fatherhood. His and Khaltinaht's eldest daughter Elizabeth claimed she was born in 1867, but it may have been a year earlier. There is no question as to the month and day of Elizabeth's birth. "Father told me that I was born on the Fourth of July. It was an American Day, and they were having a celebration at New Westminster." Portuguese Joe was as proud as any new father could be. "Father had a big time that day; treated his friends with brandy, because he had a baby girl, and that was the day I was born." Joe later told his eldest daughter how he had got "a bottle of brandy, a big barrel of beer, and invited the hand loggers." These were the men who cut down trees by hand for the sawmills that now operated on both sides of Burrard Inlet.

Precisely where Portuguese Joe and Khaltinaht were living at the time of Elizabeth's birth is unclear. Not until October 3, 1878, was the Galiano preemption "cancelled for cessation of occupation," but it seems unlikely the family lived there very long, if at all. Joe probably camped there while fishing in Georgia Strait.

The family chose to live on Burrard Inlet. A contemporary who worked at Hastings Mill on the south shore of the inlet described Portuguese Joe as "a fisherman" who had his own house on the beach but not his own landing. Joe used a flat-bottomed sailboat to fish "out in the body of the Inlet, and in English Bay." He landed his catch "just on the shore," "simply on the shore, the best part of the shore he could find." Joe "was a dog fisher, he fished dog fish for oil." A fellow fisherman explained that Joe caught dogfish on a sand bank off of Point Grey. These he took to Deadman's Island just south of Brockton Point. He put them in a "great big kettle" to boil the oil out of them. The oil he sold to a sawmill for "25¢—that was the price—per gallon for the dog fish oil for use on their machinery, or logging skid roads."

Portuguese Joe was ambitious for his young family. He wanted to expand his fishing activities. As a British subject he could acquire land, but that did not mean it would be granted to him. On May 15, 1868, "Joseph Silvy" signed with his mark a letter that began: "Being desirous of starting a fishery at Burrard Inlet I respectfully request that a lease of 20 acres on the Government Reserve inside the first narrows may be granted me (at a small rental) having a water frontage of 20 chains as shewn in the annexed sketch. I shall be prepared to leave at the shortest notice whenever the Government may require the land." The accompanying map indicated that the location was the southern shore of Brockton Point, whose sandy beach was ideal for hauling up fishing boats. Joe was not successful in his request. Officials responded that "it is not considered advisable at present to grant a lease to any portion of this Reserve." The "government reserve" designation for what would become Stanley Park harked back to the first years of the gold rush. The land was set aside so that its heights could be fortified should the mainland colonial capital of New Westminster be attacked by the expansionist United States.

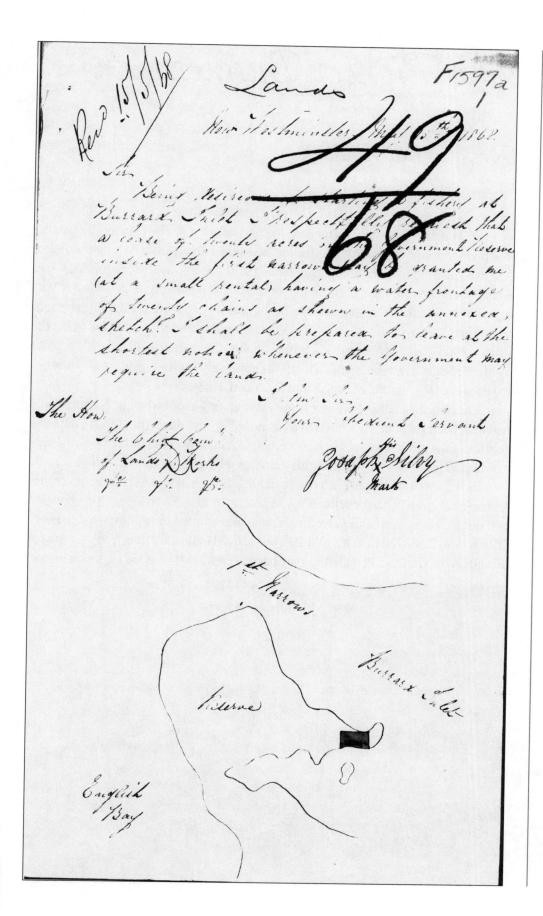

Joe's application to lease fishing grounds on the southern shore of Brockton Point, in what is now Stanley Park, was rejected by government officials who wrote that it was "considered inadvisable" to grant a lease for any part of their government preserve.
BC Archives GR1372

The Pioneer Businessman

Returning to Whaling

Joe was not easily deterred. He set off on a new adventure.

In March 1886, when Portuguese Joe had talked with the crew of the passing schooner about his fishing adventures, he mused about what he might do next. "He was thinking of going into whale fishing in the inlet—as they abounded," said a crew member. "He was going to use rockets." This passing remark indicates Portuguese Joe's considerable knowledge of the industry. The rocket-driven harpoon, sometimes known as the "rocket," contained an explosive device intended to kill the whale, unlike traditional harpoons, which hooked the animal until it could be killed by other means. The technology, which was never very successful, was only then being tried out by a handful of British and American whalers.

It is not surprising that Portuguese Joe was thinking about whaling. Native people had long been harpooning whales as they moved up and down the British Columbia coast, and the profit appeared to be enormous. A single whale could yield as much as a thousand gallons of oil, which at this time was selling for up to 50¢ a gallon.

Whaling was a far tougher job than catching dogfish. It was too big an adventure for one man, even Portuguese Joe Silvey, to take on by himself. So Joe got together with two others, Harry Trim and Peter Smith, who also wanted to capture whales. Harry Trim was an Englishman in his mid-20s, just arrived in Burrard Inlet from six years of mining in the Cariboo. Peter Smith may have been friends with Joe for much longer.

Portuguese Joe and his friends persuaded the legendary Abel Douglas to join them in starting up a small whaling camp on Pasley Island. They used his schooner, possibly the *Kate*, shown here, to tow their catch back to camp.
BC Archives H-02689

Peter was also born in the Azores and, like Joe, was in his mid-30s. They may have jumped ship together and been part of the group frightened off from the goldfields. Considerable trouble was taken during these years to track down and punish deserters, to make them examples and discourage others. It was likely Peter's fear of being caught that caused him to change his Portuguese name to just plain "Peter Smith." Sometimes he was known as Peter the Whaler or Portuguese Pete. Both Harry and Peter married Squamish women.

The three men had a plan. They had seen bleached whale bones lying on the eastern beaches of tiny Pasley Island, located to the west of larger Bowen Island, which was off the north shore of Burrard Inlet. The men knew that Native whalers towed their catch to the nearest shore, so the pods of whales that went up and down Georgia Strait must be passing by Pasley Island. That was where they decided to establish their camp.

Joe, Harry and Peter needed a vessel big enough for whaling, and they had their eye on a schooner captained by Abel Douglas, a Scot from Maine via California. Douglas had been in his late 20s in 1868 when he was enticed north from San Francisco by businessmen wanting to develop coastal whaling out of Victoria. He and his crew whaled quite successfully from Saanich Inlet, not far from Victoria, and the next year he went as far north as a site known as Whaletown on Cortes Island. Abel was ready for a new challenge, and the adventure began.

Whaling was a family affair at the Pasley "whaling camp," as recalled by Elizabeth Silvey. "Harry Trim's wife was an Indian; Peter Smith's wife was an Indian; and my father's wife was an Indian; all had little houses, nice little houses, and they built the wharf for the schooner to land. It was a nice bay... they got a lot of oil out of the whales." Abel Douglas's wife Maria Mahoi was, Portuguese Joe's daughter recalled, "half Indian and half Hawaiian." She was also part of the adventure.

Whaling imprinted itself in Elizabeth Silvey's mind. Her description from her memories as a small child makes it clear that the process was very like what it had been a generation earlier, except that the blubber was boiled on land rather than on the ship itself.

Abel Douglas's wife Maria Mahoi, whom Joe's daughter Elizabeth recalled as being "half Indian and half Hawaiian," was one of the women who lived at the whaling camp on Pasley Island. Salt Spring Archives

> I can remember Capt Douglas's big schooner coming in... I saw them bring one whale in. They were towing it. And all the people looked out and said, "Here they come." And they were towing it. We saw the schooner coming full sail, and they were towing something white. They were coming fast with all the sails. And they were towing this big thing behind the schooner. Yes. And when they turned it over it was black, and when they turned it back again it was white. They had a little wharf, and the schooner docked there; it was piles, small piles, and a pretty good little wharf. And then they had a great big cable as big as my arm; the cable was rope. They lowered the

Opposite top: On Pasley Island the whalers reduced the blubber by boiling it in large vats. The same technique was used by whaling ships at sea. © Copyright New Bedford Whaling Museum

Opposite bottom: Gastown was named after "Gassy Jack" Deighton, a contemporary of Joe's who opened the first saloon on Carrall Street for thirsty millworkers. BC Archives D-07873

Below: Portuguese Joe's daughter Elizabeth vividly remembered how the men used a windlass to haul the whale onto the beach and a "great big knife" to butcher it. As this photograph, taken at Kyuquot in 1916 shows, similar methods were still in use 30 years later. BC Archives A-09221

whaleboat; they always packed the whaleboat on the schooner, and when they saw a whale they lowered the whaleboat. And then had a big line, like a cable, and a harpoon. And then, finally, they had a big shed where they had the iron pots, you know, where they boil the blubber, the fat, and they had the harpoon on the whale's head. And then they hauled it up to the shed… They had a big thing (a windlass) right on the shore; edge of the water, and two men kept going around and around, walking around the big thing. And the rope was coming in, and bringing the whale up; it was a slow job. And then they cut the whale up with a great big knife, ready to boil; all the fat. It was all chopped up in squares, and the fat *that* thick [gesticulating to show a thickness of about 12 inches]; it was all fat; just excepting the ribs, very fat.

At the time Joe and Khaltinaht's second child was born, likely in the spring of 1871, everyone was busy whaling. "My father, Peter Smith and Harry Trim, and a Captain Douglas were whaling. Captain Douglas had a schooner and there were some more men." Young Elizabeth never forgot her sister's birth. "When she was born I was taken out of the house by Mrs. Peter Smith and Mrs. Harry Trim. They took me out that night to stay in their house on Pasley Island, and when I came back in the morning there was a baby on the bed; a little baby, and it was Josephine. And I tried to pull it off so as to have it walk with me like a doll, and they told me I could not do that; that it could not walk yet."

The whaling boom was too good to last. The industry collapsed at about the time Josephine was born. Not only were fewer whales turning up, but the price of oil fell—for some 12 years, ground oil had been extracted from sites in the Unites States. Some whaling continued on a smaller scale, but it was no longer the profitable business it had once been.

Keeping a Saloon

Perhaps because whaling was seasonal, or because Portuguese Joe was by nature active and ambitious, he embarked on yet another adventure even before he had stopped whaling. He became a businessman.

Burrard Inlet was a hive of activity, with booming sawmills and a brisk shipping business. The need for a variety of goods and services was growing, and small businesses were springing up all along the south shore of the inlet, near where Portuguese Joe and his family lived. The community was called Gastown, after a saloon owned and operated by John "Gassy Jack" Deighton, a colourful Yorkshire seaman who like so many others had been enticed to British Columbia by the gold rush. He arrived at Burrard Inlet in September 1867, and a contemporary, Thomas Fisher, recalled how "I helped him build the first saloon, which was a little shack of a place [that] stood right on Carrall Street."

Like many other European men, Gassy Jack had a Native wife, and the story goes that on her death he purchased "for a larger price" her 12-year-old niece Whahalia. Perhaps because the exchange did not fit the image he wished to project in the community, he secreted Madeleine, as he called her, "in a little cabin back in the forest, to which he retreated for peace and quietness." Joe's daughter Elizabeth once mused, "I remember her when I was about five years old; gee, she was a pretty lady."

Among the other Gastown businesses was a general store that served both millworkers and local Natives, who could land their canoes on the long float jutting out from the store and trade furs for other goods. The store's owner was another Portuguese man, Gregorio Fernandez, who had come from the island of Madeira. A former

Portuguese Joe opened his saloon, Hole-in-the-Wall (visible at the end of the block) at the corner of Water and Abbott streets. Near the big maple tree was Deighton's bar, while across the street was Gregorio Fernandez's store.
City of Vancouver Archives, CVA Dist. P11.1

Cariboo miner, he may have been one of the men with whom Joe Silvey jumped ship. Joe's daughter Elizabeth referred affectionately to Fernandez, who also went by the nickname "Portuguese Joe," as her uncle, although he was not a blood relative. Another of Joe Silvey's children recalled that Fernandez "had gold earrings; I saw them myself; it was an old custom with sailor men."

With Fernandez's encouragement, Portuguese Joe opened a saloon that, like Gassy Jack's down the street, catered to millworkers. The exact periods during which it operated are unclear. Joe got a new licence in January 1870, only to shut his doors in mid-year, "owing to the mill being closed." On December 15, 1870, he requested permission to reopen, pointing out to the government official in charge of licensing: "I pay my rent and all government dues. I have built a saloon and paid for the ground and I should like to have my licence the same as before and the property is no account to me without the licence." Although one of his competitors was allowed to reopen, Joe's request was refused because of the "opposition of the agent of the Hastings Mill Company." The new mill manager, who was staunchly religious, considered such activity suspect and did not want any more saloons in operation than absolutely necessary.

At about this time Portuguese Joe got an opportunity to purchase the land on which his saloon stood. The area extending from Hastings Street north to Burrard Inlet and from Carrall east to Cambie Street—officially named Granville, although still informally known as Gastown—was surveyed and the survey was registered on March 1, 1870. Colonial regulations stated that town land, once surveyed, had to be offered for sale at auction. A land sale was held on April 11. Gassy Jack bought his property and Gregorio Fernandez purchased the land at the northwest corner of Water and Abbott streets on which his general store stood. Portuguese Joe did not follow suit. Perhaps he was out whaling; more likely the business climate was stagnant. Not until a year later, on May 9, 1871, did Joe buy Lot 7 of Block 2, located at the southeast corner of Water and Abbott streets, for $100. By then he must have reopened his saloon, which he called the Hole-in-the-Wall.

Two Worlds of Childhood

Joseph Silvey's ability to move between the fishing traditions he had absorbed from his childhood and the entrepreneurial ethos of Burrard Inlet was impressive. Equally so was the capacity of his eldest daughter Elizabeth to manoeuvre between the very different worlds of her parents. Even as an elder she retained vivid memories of both the raw frontier society of her father and the centuries-old aboriginal culture of her mother.

The Silveys lived in a house that Joe built near the saloon, so his business became a part of young Elizabeth's everyday life. "Father always had gold and silver. I've seen it in a little sack; no bills. That was when he had that little saloon in 'Gastown.' I saw it on the counter. And no one would ever touch it. He was putting out the rum; reaching up to the shelf for a bottle, and the men were all standing drinking in his saloon, and the money—he was making change. Them days they had gold and silver, no bills." She remembered all the bottles on the shelf, "and there was a counter. It was on the Gastown beach, and the street was just planked over." Her adopted uncle was a favourite. "I remember running over to Joe [i.e. Gregorio] Fernandez's store across from our place—just a few steps—nearly every day. The men who came into the bar room used to give me 10¢, or 50¢, and I used to run over to Joe's store and get candy. Joe Fernandez had a great big cordwood stove in the store; I used to stand by it when I went over to get candy from Joe."

Elizabeth described the special events that took place in that tiny community hugging the south shore of Burrard Inlet. "They used to have lots of fun at Christmas and Halloween in Gastown. The men used to dress up and put on long white whiskers, and at Halloween put on masks. Oh, yes, I remember it; it used to be delightful for the children." There were dances or at least musical evenings, at which "Father played the violin, guitar, and the mandolin."

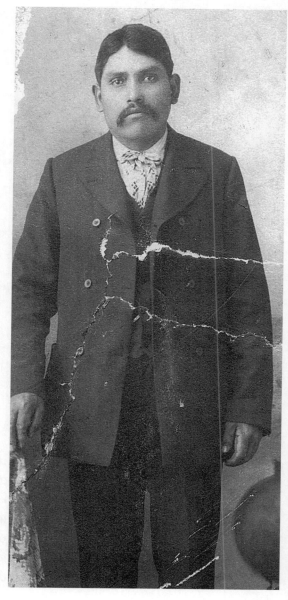

When the Silveys lived in Gastown, they counted among their many friends Joe Thomas, "a full-blood Indian" who married Khaltinaht's sister Lumtinaht. City of Vancouver Archives, Port P393

Elizabeth's mother Khaltinaht was especially close to her sister Lumtinaht, also known as Louise, whom she resembled closely. Lumtinaht married Joe Thomas, recalled as a "full-blood Indian," whereas their half-sister Rowia wed "Navvy Jack" Thomas. John Thomas was another Englishman lured to British Columbia by the gold rush. Having made some money from mining he headed to Burrard Inlet. In 1866, with lumber mills now operating on both sides of the inlet, Navvy Jack started ferrying passengers and their goods between them.

Portuguese Joe's wife Khaltinaht is said to have closely resembled her sister Lumtinaht, whose noble position in her tribe afforded her an honoured role during potlatches at Musqueam and at Whoi Whoi. City of Vancouver Archives, CVA Port P392

Navvy Jack settled his family in a small cottage on the north shore, perhaps to be closer to Rowia's grandfather, Chief Kiapilano. According to his eldest daughter Christine, "he was very fond of gardening and grew tobacco and sugar cane in his garden." For a long time Navvy Jack and his family were the only newcomers in what is today West Vancouver. At the same time, he remained an adventurer, and from time to time he returned to the Cariboo to try his luck once more. Christine told about her father's "good family," who begged him repeatedly to return home, or at least send his children to England to be educated, but he would never forgive his mother for the quarrel that caused him to leave in the first place. Like his brother-in-law Portuguese Joe, Navvy Jack did not look back but rather forward to the possibilities that British Columbia had to offer.

Khaltinaht's aboriginal world became an integral part of Elizabeth's own. Khaltinaht, her sister Lumtinaht and the young child spent much time together. One of the events recalled most vividly by Elizabeth in her old age was a large potlatch that was held in 1870 at Whoi Whoi, the Squamish village of which her great-uncle was chief. Whoi Whoi was located at what is now Lumberman's Arch in Stanley Park. An early Methodist minister described Whoi Whoi during these years: "As a side trip I frequently took a rowboat or canoe to the First Narrows to visit a small band living in Stanley Park where the Lumberman's Arch now stands…The biggest community house there was probably 100 feet long by 40 feet wide. The Indians did not live in separate homes, but in one long community house."

Because Lumtinaht was related to the chief, she played a special role at potlatches. "Lumtinaht was the 'princess' or 'queen' that they had at the potlatches, all over; sometimes at Musqueam, sometimes at Whoi Whoi." Lumtinaht's role was carefully circumscribed. "Before the potlatch started they had a great pile of blankets, and they got a [girl of] 'high' station to sit on it. That was part of the ceremony. To show that they had the blankets, I suppose. She, the princess, was my aunt; my mother's sister…It would be improper to have a common girl sit on the blankets; they had a great pile of them, and a princess sitting on top…The blankets were all in a pile, and the seat on top of them was the seat of honour."

"I was little, but I can remember [that potlatch] clearly," Elizabeth said.

My mother took me to it on her back; she "packed" me to it, and when we got near there were "thousands" of Indians…and I was frightened. I didn't know who gave the potlatch, but I think my grandmother's brother…They held the potlatch in a great big shed, a huge place; the Indians built it themselves long ago…There was no floor; just earth, and the fires were all burning…The platforms were high up, inside, of course, and the chiefs were away up on the platform, and throwing blankets and money down, and those below scrambling for it. Mother took me, on her back, but when they began to dance and throw money about, I got frightened, and ran. I darted through under their legs, in and out in the crowd, and dashed out of the building; I didn't wait for anyone; not even mother; she came after me, and had to take me home; she could not stop at the potlatch because I was so frightened.

Elizabeth was also taken to visit Khaltinaht's grandparents. Chief Kiapilano lived on the north shore of Burrard Inlet at the village of Homulcheson. "He was kind, and nice. I was a little girl then," she remembered. "When I was about three years old…my mother took me over to the Indian houses at Capilano Creek, and there I saw old chief Kiapilano; a great big old man with big legs, and loud voice…and long white hair hanging down over his shoulders; down to his shoulder blades, and the ends used to curl upwards; he was short-sighted." All her life Elizabeth retained fond memories of her great-grandfather.

Turned Upside Down

Portuguese Joe Silvey had worked hard since coming to British Columbia. By 1871, when the colony of British Columbia became a province of the new Dominion of Canada, he could take very real satisfaction in his accomplishments. Joe had a growing family and more than one way of making a living. He was still whaling, he fished, and he owned the property on which his saloon stood. Everything seemed to be turning out right.

Then Portuguese Joe's world turned upside down. His wife Khaltinaht grew ill and died. "She caught cold in her back, I gathered from remarks my father dropped, when my little sister was born," Elizabeth remembered, "and my little sister was less than a year old when Mother died…I must have been about four years old." Khaltinaht told Joe that in death she wanted to be returned to her people, and so it was. "She wanted to be buried at Musqueam, so she was buried there…I remember my mother dying in Gastown, and how her people at Musqueam came for her body, and took it in a canoe for burial at Musqueam."

Joe was devastated. "My father was left with two young children, one unable to walk," Elizabeth said. He could no longer bear to live in Gastown, so "he sold the saloon to some hand loggers."

Starting Over

Now in middle age, Portuguese Joe Silvey started all over again. He retreated to the site at Brockton Point that he had tried, unsuccessfully, to lease for a fishing camp. It is likely that the family already lived there from time to time, perhaps on a seasonal basis, but now they moved permanently. "Father sold out and went to live at Brockton Point," Elizabeth explained. "He put up a house there, near Deadman's Island, facing east." To make a living for his family, Joe returned, at least for a time, to the business he knew best and got a licence to run a saloon at Brockton Point.

The Silveys' new house was not far from Whoi Whoi, where Khaltinaht's people had their longhouse and where Elizabeth had been taken to the big potlatch from which she ran away. Joe maintained a close relationship with his wife's family, and Elizabeth recalled how "Great-grandfather Chief Kiapilano used to come and camp at Brockton Point; in a tent in front of our house, and I used to see him resting on his bed in the tent." From her perspective as a small child: "He was a great big man with a voice like a microphone on a loudspeaker; he spoke loud. Anyway, that's how it seemed to me; I was little. And he had long white hair; it was bobbed, and white, and he always had a smile. He beckoned to me to come to him, and I would not go, but afterwards I did, and he took me up in one arm, and held me to his breast. Oh, he was a nice man; everyone liked him." According to Elizabeth, "Chief Kiapilano had lots of wives...used to visit them every month." On his visits to Brockton Point, "he had a hunchback slave wife to look after him; I used to visit him constantly in that old tent."

Elizabeth found a friend near her own age at Brockton Point. "Tomkins Brew was living at Brockton Point when we went there; he had quite a nice little cottage; it was about 20 feet or so...on that little bit of clearing right on that little point." He was an Irishman in his mid-30s and worked as the constable and customs collector at Burrard Inlet. Tomkins Brew and his Native wife were the parents of Arthur, who was a little older than Elizabeth.

Devastated by the loss of his beloved Khaltinaht, Portuguese Joe left Gastown and moved with his two young daughters to the small community at Brockton Point, where he built a house just across the water from Deadman's Island.
BC Archives D-04722

Several other families lived nearby. Peter Smith had settled down in a ménage that included, next door to him, his wife Kenick's father Shwutchalton. According to Portuguese Pete's eldest daughter Mary, he built a house of "old split cedar," put a fence around it and constructed a float that extended out into the water. Johnny Baker was an Englishman who had likely also jumped ship. He and his Squamish wife Tsiyaliya had two sons, Johnny and Willie, and four daughters. Some indigenous Hawaiians, or Kanakas as they were called in the fur trade, lived south of Brockton Point at what was called Coal Harbour. Eihu, Nahanee and the others went by canoe to their jobs at Hastings Mill.

Life on Brockton Point had some practical disadvantages for young Elizabeth. Whereas Arthur Brew attended the small school at Hastings Sawmill, to the east of Brockton Point, Elizabeth was too little to do so. "I never went to the Hastings Sawmill school…but I remember Arthur Brew, son of Tomkins Brew; he was a big boy going to school." All the same, Elizabeth learned a lot of practical skills from her father, including boat building. Thinking back to his early years in the Azores, Portuguese Joe decided that he wanted his own *Morning Star*. "Father built a sloop; I helped him; he built it at Brockton Point. I was only a little girl but I could hold the boards and I could hand him the nails, and could hold something against the other side of the board when he was hammering; put a little pressure on."

With the *Morning Star*, Portuguese Joe could venture farther afield along the British Columbia coast. He must have gone north from Burrard Inlet and even considered settling there, for on May 28, 1872, "Joseph Silvia Seamens" preempted 160 acres on Howe Sound.

Among the Silveys' friends was Ada Guinne, whose French-Canadian father farmed at Marpole and whose mother was Khaltinaht's aunt. Wed to Peter Plant, a French Canadian man, in 1866 at Moodyville, she was recorded as "Burrard Inlet's first bride."
City of Vancouver Archives
CVA Port P714

Rebuilding a Family

Portuguese Joe's first task in rebuilding his family was to find a wife and mother for his two daughters. "Josephine wasn't a year old; that's why Father got married again," Elizabeth said. "Two little girls and no one to look after them." It is likely that Joe was sailing on the *Morning Star* up Georgia Strait along the Sechelt Peninsula when he met Kwahama Kwatleematt, whose Christian name was Lucy. They were married in Sechelt.

Times had changed since Joe Silvey wed Khaltinaht in the traditions of her people. Missionaries had spent years convincing the Natives that they should be married in the "white" style. Lucy may have been educated by the Oblates, who had ministered at Sechelt since the early 1860s, for she knew how to read and write—unusual skills for a young Native woman at the time.

Lucy was just 15 and Portuguese Joe almost three times her age when, on September 20, 1872, Father Paul Durieu of the Oblate order married them in the Catholic mission church at Sechelt. They were both very properly dressed, Joe in a suit, vest and tie, his handlebar moustache neatly trimmed for the occasion, and Lucy in an elegant dress with her hair demurely pulled back. Lucy's parents, Andrew Kwakoil and Agatha, likely looked on. Elizabeth, who was about five at the time, recalled: "We went up in the *Morning Star*. I wasn't at the wedding; I was too young and small for that, but I was there and saw what was going on, and so was Josephine. Josephine was just a little thing."

Joe's new family returned to Brockton Point for at least part of each year. When he got married, Joe described himself as a fisherman, and he spent much of the time on the *Morning Star*. "He always used to go around fishing," Elizabeth recalled, "and we stayed at home in the house he built; he built a little house." Other times the family went with him. They travelled north up the Georgia Strait to Pender Harbour on the Sechelt Peninsula, across to Vancouver Island and the coal-mining town of Nanaimo and to nearby Newcastle Island, and spent time in "a bay by the lighthouse on Gabriola Island." Joe was coming to know the coast very well.

It was during these years, according to Elizabeth, that Joe Silvey pioneered seine fishing in British Columbia, building on practices he had learned as a young man. "Father taught the Indian women how to knit nets at Brockton Point; taught them how to make seine nets, and then he used to stain the nets in vats, and then they

Unlike Joe's first wedding, which was celebrated with a traditional Native ceremony, his second marriage was recognized by government officials in New Westminster.
BC Archives, Vital Statistics

Joe's second wife was Kwahama Kwatleematt, or Lucy, a Sechelt woman a third his age. They celebrated their marriage by having their photograph taken.
Courtesy Jessica Casey

went out on the little bit of sandy beach, facing this way from Brockton Point, and used to catch herrings. One would go away out in the boat with one end, and one away out with the other end, and then they would circle around, and two men on one rope end and two men on the other end would pull the net slowly, slowly, into the sandy beach, and they would get—well, I heard them say there was a ton of herrings in the net, you could see the net coming in with the herring all splashing in it; drawing it up on the beach." Elizabeth remembered that her father was the first man in British Columbia "to have a seine licence to fish," or at least to have "the first herring seine licence." A younger sister recalled, perhaps referring to a later point in time, how "my father Portuguese Joe Silvey used to have gill nets and rent them out to the Indians and every Indian on the coast knew him."

It was important not only to catch the fish, but to make a living by doing so. "They used to put the herrings in barrels, and they used to salt it; they used to sell them to the schooners [which were in port to load spars and lumber]. The schooners used to come in, and get 100 barrels each, and go away; sometimes as much as 150 barrels." Joe used some of the herring for bait to catch dogfish up the coast. One of his grandsons said that Joe went as far north as Cowichan Gap, later renamed Porlier Pass, between Galiano and Valdes islands. Elizabeth recalled his going to "Pender Harbour, where they were fishing for dogfish, and Capt Douglas was there, too, fishing for dog-

Portuguese Joe is credited with pioneering seine fishing in British Columbia. His daughter Elizabeth recalled him teaching Native women how to knit nets at Brockton Point. Vancouver Public Library, Special Collections, VPL 54781

fish. And they sold their oil to Nanaimo and Departure Bay [coal mines]." The early Vancouver historian Alan Morley termed Silvey "a prosperous manufacturer of dog-fish oil for the mills and logging camps."

Portuguese Joe worked as a fisherman for wages during part of each year, taking Lucy and the children with him. Two Englishmen, Alexander Ewen and James Wise, were among the first entrepreneurs to use the new tin can technology to export salmon. They opened their first cannery on the Fraser River in 1870. "Ewen and Wise, at Westminster used to call my father the 'net boss' during the summer fishing season; we used to live in the boathouse by Mr. Wise's store in New Westminster," Elizabeth recalled. "Mr. Ewen, the canneryman" once sent for her father, and the family went to New Westminster by rowboat, with a stop along the way at the farm of Quebecer Supplien Guinne to "get some butter and eggs." Guinne's wife was Chief Kiapilano's sister, hence young Elizabeth's great aunt.

Other men living at Brockton Point also fished, including some of the Hawaiians. "You know, there were a lot of Kanakas about, not just one or two, and they would talk in their language; it was queer to hear them, and they would go out where the light-house is at Brockton Point and fish with a line." Lucy, Elizabeth's stepmother, took her along to buy vegetables from Eihu's Squamish wife Mary See-em-ia, who "lived down at the little ranch at Coal Harbour," a short canoe ride from Brockton Point. Kanaka Ranch, as it was called, was at the foot of today's Denman Street.

"It was quite a profitable undertaking—fishing," Elizabeth recalled much later. "I remember some of the 'Gastown' men joking about going to give up store keeping and lumbering, and go fishing; there was money in fishing; lots of money in it." Joe Silvey helped to make fishing a viable and attractive occupation in British Columbia.

Whenever the work was over, Joe would return home to his new family at Brockton Point. Joe's first son Domingo was born on August 10, 1874. His daughter Mary was, according to her own recollection, "born in Stanley Park, just across from Deadman's Island, May 24th 1877." She explained how "they used to call me 'the Queen' because I was born on the 24th May, the Queen[Victoria]'s birthday."

All of the children retained special memories of Brockton Point. Mary "used to climb up in the boughs of the Maple tree, and drop little pebbles on people I did not like who passed underneath; used to climb up there, and stay up in the branches all day when they were looking for me to give me a hiding; used to take a pocket of pebbles up there with me." She remembered "Tomkins Brew, and the little Customs office; he had a long beard, and used to nurse me; I did not like him very well." Elizabeth recalled: "Tomkins Brew had an Indian wife; big fine beautiful woman, and he was fond of her. But she got sick, and I can see him yet, with his arm around her neck as she was lying there in her bed; but she did not get better, and she died."

It was not just the families at Brockton Point who visited back and forth. A number of families around Burrard Inlet besides the Silveys consisted of newcomer white men and Native women. For immigrants of British or white Canadian descent who arrived later and saw themselves at the centre of the emerging dominant society,

Portuguese Joe often stopped in Nanaimo to sell some of his dogfish oil to the local coal mines. BC Archives A-04429

In the summers, Joe and his family sometimes lived in a boathouse at the Ewen and Wise cannery on the Fraser River at New Westminster.
Vancouver Public Library,
VPL 1788

racial hybridity was inherently suspect, as was anyone of an ethnic background different from their own. Thomas Bryant, the son of an early Methodist minister, replied to a request for information in the 1930s that "I did not know Gregorio Fernandez nor any of their kind— or any of the Portuguese gents."

Likely in part for that reason, a lively social life joined Portuguese Joe and his family with others like themselves spread across Burrard Inlet and on the islands that dotted the strait between the inlet and Vancouver Island. Thanks to Joe's fishing and whaling expeditions, he was so familiar with the coast that it was almost like his hometown, the water its main street. Khaltinaht's sister Rowia and her husband Navvy Jack Thomas lived in what later became West Vancouver. On the property east of Navvy Jack's was William Bridge, described by an early settler of North Vancouver as "an English sailor who had left his ship." Bridge was already living there with his Native wife in 1869 when he preempted 160 acres at the foot of today's Chesterfield Avenue. As well as a "cottage of board and batten with cedar shake roof," Bridge "planted orchard, made little garden, created a pasture for cows, made splendid little farm, and sold milk." Elizabeth Silvey recalled, "I used to play with his children at the north shore, when we went over there."

John Silva had been born at about the same time as Portuguese Joe. According to Silva's descendants, the two men jumped ship together. Silva worked for a time on coastal steamers, and by 1863 was operating a fruit and vegetable store in Victoria. He wanted more, and in 1873 he took up land on Mayne Island. Shortly thereafter he married Louisa, the 15-year-old daughter of a Cowichan chief. The story that has been passed down in the family has John Silva giving his future in-laws "two horses hitched and ready for working—two horses and about three sacks of spuds." This arrangement, like other cross-cultural unions, was difficult at first, as described by Louisa's granddaughter Margaret. "She was really frightened of marriage, you know, how it would be, so she was given part of the boat and she was crying away and my grandfather was kind and gentle and he took her to his log cabin on Mayne Island and Mother said that it was a dirt floor—a log cabin—and Mother said that Grandpa said, 'well, the first thing you have to do, Louisa, is to make a batch of bread because we do not have any bread,' so he got the fire going [and when] she was making that bread she was crying into the dough."

John Silva fished and Louisa bore the children, 10 of them. Like his friend Portuguese Joe, John Silva soon decided that there was no turning back. On June 27, 1876, he took his oath as a British subject, which entitled him to own outright the land on which they lived. A few years later, in the early 1880s, the Silva family moved from Mayne to Gabriola Island because of persistent Native raiding parties on their sheep. According to their granddaughter Margaret, "The Haida Indians kept coming through the passageway and they'd hoot and they'd holler and away they would come and they were a pretty fearful bunch and my grandfather kept sheep and he had goats and he had geese and stuff and these Indians would come through and they'd take about half of his stuff to feed their families—I guess they didn't like to live on fish all the time!—and anyway my grandmother decided, 'I am not living here,' so she said to my grandfather, 'I want to get out of here,' and so she talked him into moving to Gabriola Island."

Among the other Portuguese people who settled nearby were the Bittancourt brothers, John Norton and John Enos. Estalon and Manuel Bittancourt came from the Azores via the Australian gold rush of the early 1850s. Sometime thereafter they persuaded their fellow Azorean John Norton to join them on Salt Spring Island, located west of Galiano where Portuguese Joe had once held land. João Inacio, who simplified his name to John Enos, also came from the Azores. Like the others, he had gone to sea in his early teens. He jumped ship at Boston in 1852 and worked his way west to California, hoping to get rich from gold. He found all the good claims staked, and he made his way north to British Columbia as soon as he got news of the gold rush there. He tells a story of being scared away by Native people at Yale that is so similar to Portuguese Joe's account, it's very possible that they made the trip together. John Enos got work near Nanaimo, took up land a bit farther north at Nanoose Bay in 1863, and married a Songhees woman whom he named Teresa Elisia. Just as the Bittancourts and Norton had done, Enos acquired a reputation as a successful farmer. When Portuguese Joe and his family travelled on the *Morning Star*, they very likely stopped in to visit their countrymen.

One More Adventure

Perhaps it was the visits the Silveys made to families who lived on their own island or bay that inspired one more adventure. Having fished up and down the coast on the *Morning Star*, Portuguese Joe wondered whether a location other than Brockton Point might offer a better life to his growing family. More and more newcomers were settling on Burrard Inlet, bringing with them racist attitudes that were generally accepted whence they had come. Natives were scorned and persons of mixed race denigrated as "half-breeds." Portuguese Joe could recall the "old days" at Point Roberts and Gastown, when everyone was accepted on their merits as opposed to the accident of birth.

Joe's home in what is today Stanley Park was no longer the safe haven it had once been. Even though he was refused permission to lease the land on which his family lived, he and the others had been mostly left alone. But times were changing. During the mid-1870s the federal government, which had taken responsibility for Native people when British Columbia became a province of Canada in 1871, made a big

In 1913 a large wooden "Lumberman's Arch," built for a Royal visit to Vancouver, was erected where the village of Whoi Whoi had stood for centuries. City of Vancouver Archives, CVA Arch P40

effort to confine them to reserves. Officials visited the long-time Squamish village of Whoi Whoi, which they preferred to believe had followed rather than preceded the newcomers' arrival. "These Indians have squatted on the Govt. Reserve between Coal Harbor and the First Narrows," wrote the British Columbia Reserve Commission in November 1876. "They have several small cottages but have made little improvement otherwise."

At this point the authorities had no interest in the other families living nearby, but Joe and his neighbours might well have wondered what would happen next. Once again Portuguese Joe Silvey pulled up stakes. He sold his Gastown property, and passed their Brockton Point home on to Gregorio Fernandez's nephew Joe Gonsalves. "I tried to find out if my father sold it to Gonsalves," recalled Elizabeth, "but from what I could learn he did not; he just left it." Fernandez brought his nephew out from Madeira in 1874 to become his heir, for he was ill, and a year later he died. "There was a drunken brawl, or fight, and Fernandez got mixed up in it, somehow, and got a cut on the leg, and gangrene set in; he died. I was a little girl, but I can just remember it. I think he was put in jail at [New] Westminster, and died there." Joe Gonsalves went on to make his living as a fisherman at Brockton Point until 1904. In that year he bought out the general store at Irvines Landing, at Pender Harbour on the Sechelt Peninsula, where some of his descendants still live.

Reid Island

Joe Silvey's destination when he left Brockton Point was Reid Island, located northwest of Galiano Island, where he had once taken up land. About 240 acres in size, Reid Island lies at a crossroads. Immediately to the east is Porlier Pass, which runs between the much larger Galiano and Valdes islands. Thetis and Kuper islands are due west, the Vancouver Island sawmill community of Chemainus is just beyond them, Nanaimo lies to the north and Salt Spring Island lies south-southwest. Reid Island is shaped like an egg with a smaller overlapping egg at its southern end. High tide almost cuts the island in half. A dike was eventually built on the east side where the two "eggs" intersect, the diked area between the overlapping eggs being known as Mud Bay.

Joseph Silvey preempted 160 acres of Reid Island on September 19, 1881. A decade later, on May 13, 1891, his eldest son Domingo applied for "the rest of the Island more or less." Domingo's portion was designated Lots 34 and 36, Portuguese Joe's Lot 35. Father and son each wrote an *X* on the signature line.

Joe was well into middle age when he arrived on Reid Island, but he essentially started over. He built his family a house, around whose windows he ran a grapevine said to have come from Portugal—in spirit, if not literally. The house, set back from the water on the east side of the small egg, was soon complemented by an apple orchard. On Reid Island the Silvey family continued to expand. To Elizabeth, Josephine, Domingo and Mary were added seven more children, all but one of whom survived into adulthood.

The record of the Silvey children's baptisms, mostly at the Catholic mission to the Penelakut people on Kuper Island, chronicle their arrival. This record also indicates the various ways in which Portuguese Joe's surname was recorded by others as they heard him say it. Joseph was born on October 22, 1879, at Nanaimo, the son of Joseph Silvey and Lucia Cluett from Cowichan Gap. On April 30, 1882, John was born to Joseph Silvy and Lucie of Reid Island. Antonio, known as Tony, was described at his baptism on May 4, 1884, as born 15 days earlier on Reid Island to Joseph Silva and Lucia. Manuel was baptized at the age of two months on November 10, 1886, the son of Joseph Silver and Lucia. Clara Rosa Isabella, aged seven months and the daughter of Joseph Silvey and Lucia, was baptized on October 16, 1889, at home. She died in 1893 on Reid

A map of Reid Island showing how it was developed in the early 20th century.

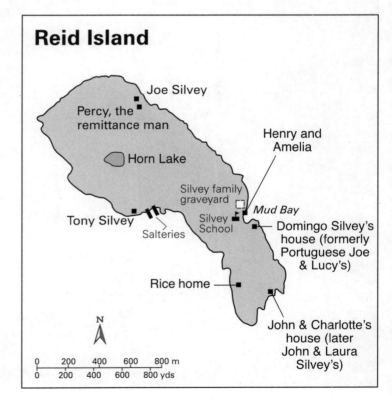

Reid Island

Joe Silvey

Percy, the remittance man

Horn Lake

Henry and Amelia

Silvey family graveyard

Mud Bay

Tony Silvey

Salteries

Silvey School

Domingo Silvey's house (formerly Portuguese Joe & Lucy's)

Rice home

John & Charlotte's house (later John & Laura Silvey's)

N

| 0 | 200 | 400 | 600 | 800 m |
| 0 | 200 | 400 | 600 | 800 yds |

Island. Andrew Trinidardi, known as Henry, was born on February 13, 1890, on Reid Island. Portuguese Joe's last child, Lena Rose, came along on April 9, 1895, on Reid Island. By then Joe was in his early 60s, Lucy in her late 30s. Portuguese Joe took great pride in his family. According to his daughter Mary, "Father had all our pictures taken; they were in tintypes; he sent them back to Portugal."

Even as children were being born, the eldest left home. Elizabeth wed not long after Portuguese Joe settled his family on Reid Island. She later claimed the marriage had occurred against her father's and her own wishes. Her 19-year-old husband James Walker was, like herself, the product of a cross-cultural union: his father was an American gold miner, his mother a Cowichan woman named Mary Sitkwa Whilemot. Shortly after James's birth, Mary married William Curran, another American enticed to British Columbia by gold. They and their growing family, which eventually totalled seven children, settled down on Thetis Island, where her family lived.

According to Elizabeth: "Mr. Walker kidnapped me; I did not know I was going to be married until I was in the little rowboat; nor did my father. James Walker asked my father if he could have me for his wife, and my father was furious about it; said 'no' that I could not be married until I was 20, and I heard him telling my stepmother that

Opposite: We owe much of our understanding of Joe's life to his eldest daughter Elizabeth who shared her recollections with Major J.S. Matthews, Vancouver's first archivist. City of Vancouver Archives, CVA 371-2397

Below: Portuguese Joe's eldest son Domingo, his wife Josephine, and their children Clara, Laura and James. Courtesy Chris Thompson

he did not want me to marry James Walker." All the same, the couple courted. "James Walker, my husband, used to come over and visit me; what they call a boyfriend now; and he asked my stepmother if he could take me out for a boat ride. So I went. I stepped into his boat and he rowed away from Reid Island; his home was on Thetis Island; he kept on rowing, and rowed over to Kuper Island, and we were married by the Rev. Mr. Roberts." Roberts ran an Anglican mission that competed with a Catholic counterpart for Penelakut souls.

Elizabeth explained how "they have it down on this marriage paper that I was 20 years old when I was married, July 15th 1883, at Kuper Island Anglican Church, but they cheated on my age, I was only 16." She described what happened. "The minister said, 'She's not 20; she's just a child,' when we went to be married, but James Walker's stepfather, he said to the minister, 'Yes she is 20,' and the minister said he did not think I was that old, and I was too young, but Curran, that's James Walker's stepfather, he said he had known me since I was a baby, which was a lie because he knew of me only since I went to Reid Island." In old age, Elizabeth bitterly regretted what happened, reflecting that "I had four children, two girls and two boys, before I was 20," her supposed age upon her marriage.

At first Elizabeth lived with her Curran in-laws on Thetis Island. Her husband did odd jobs, sometimes for the Reverend Roberts, whose diary gives a good sense of the life of an itinerant labourer, one of whom was "Jimmy Walker ($^1/_2$ Breed)." Roberts considered him a kind of superior servant. On October 22, 1883, Roberts "told Jimmy Walker to come to assist in taking off a part of our freight." Three weeks later "Jimmy Walker and his wife" Elizabeth went with Roberts to Chemainus on Vancouver Island, likely to give assistance of some kind. On January 1, 1884, "my workman, Jimmy Walker, is away [having gone with his wife to see Joe Silvey]." Walker acted as interpreter into the local Cowichan language and Roberts noted on the following Sunday: "As Jimmy Walker was not there I addressed the Congregation in Chinook." Chinook was the jargon used across the Pacific Northwest since the fur trade as a means of communication between Natives and newcomers. At the service a week later, "Jimmy

Above: Elizabeth's husband James Walker with their two oldest sons William and Frank. James Walker "kidnapped" Elizabeth while out on a date and forced her to marry him.
City of Vancouver Archives, CVA 371-2394

interpreted a short address on Luke 2:46 and then I spoke (without interpreter) for some length...The Currans & Walkers had dinner Chez nous, & went away in the evening. Before they went we had the Melodeon brought up for Singing of Hymns—& Again tonight I paid Jimmy Walker Balance due to him $5.50." Three days later, "[young Willie] Curran & Jimmy Walker came here at Noon. C. has contracted to saw 200 blocks @ 10¢ a block. They began work this P.M. and boarded Chez nous—sleeping on their sloop." By Friday, January 25: "Jimmy Walker this A.M. finished the Contract of cutting 200 blocks of wood. I paid Jimmy for his share $13.50 & also gave him for Mr Curran 2 fowl & 2 dozen eggs." At the time of the 1891 census James Walker was employed near Nanaimo as a general labourer and his wife Elizabeth worked as a servant.

Back on Reid Island, Joe Silvey continued to make a living from the sea, doing "all kinds of fishing according to the seasons—perch fishing with a small net, cod fishing with hook and line, trolling for spring and blueback salmon, clam digging night and day with low tide." According to one account, Portuguese Joe was "granted a fishing concession from Nanaimo to Sansum Narrows [between Salt Spring and Vancouver islands] to take dog and coho salmon. The dog salmon were sold to Todd's [cannery] for 2¹/2 cents each, but the coho were thrown out—the cannery wouldn't take them because they were considered too dry." In the 1901 census, Joe Silvey described himself as a fisherman who had earned $600 over the past year, a fair income for the time.

Portuguese Joe combined occupations, much as he had done earlier at Brockton Point. "Father had a little store on Reid Island, alongside of the house." The store was convenient to Porlier Pass, much used by sailing vessels along the coast. Reverend Roberts' diary entry of October 7, 1883, makes it clear that family members sometimes ran the store. "Halfway between Joe Silvia's Island & Cowichan Gap [Porlier Pass] we saw Joe. S. and [John] Norton of Ganges Harbour [on Salt Spring] hauling dog-fish from their lines...Running back to Joe's Island there was a strong wind & heavy sea. We reefed mainsail—ran into a very small cove at Joe's place. Got some provisions at his store. It was wet & stormy as we went home [to Kuper Island]."

Reverend Roberts' diary testifies to Portuguese Joe's entrepreneurial bent. Roberts wrote on April 2, 1882: "Soon after the [Sunday] Service Charlie Quiem & a white man named Silvy came to the house to get me to write out a paper (a Promissory Note). Quiem was about to lend Silvy $100 at 12 per Cent per Annum for 12 months. Geo.

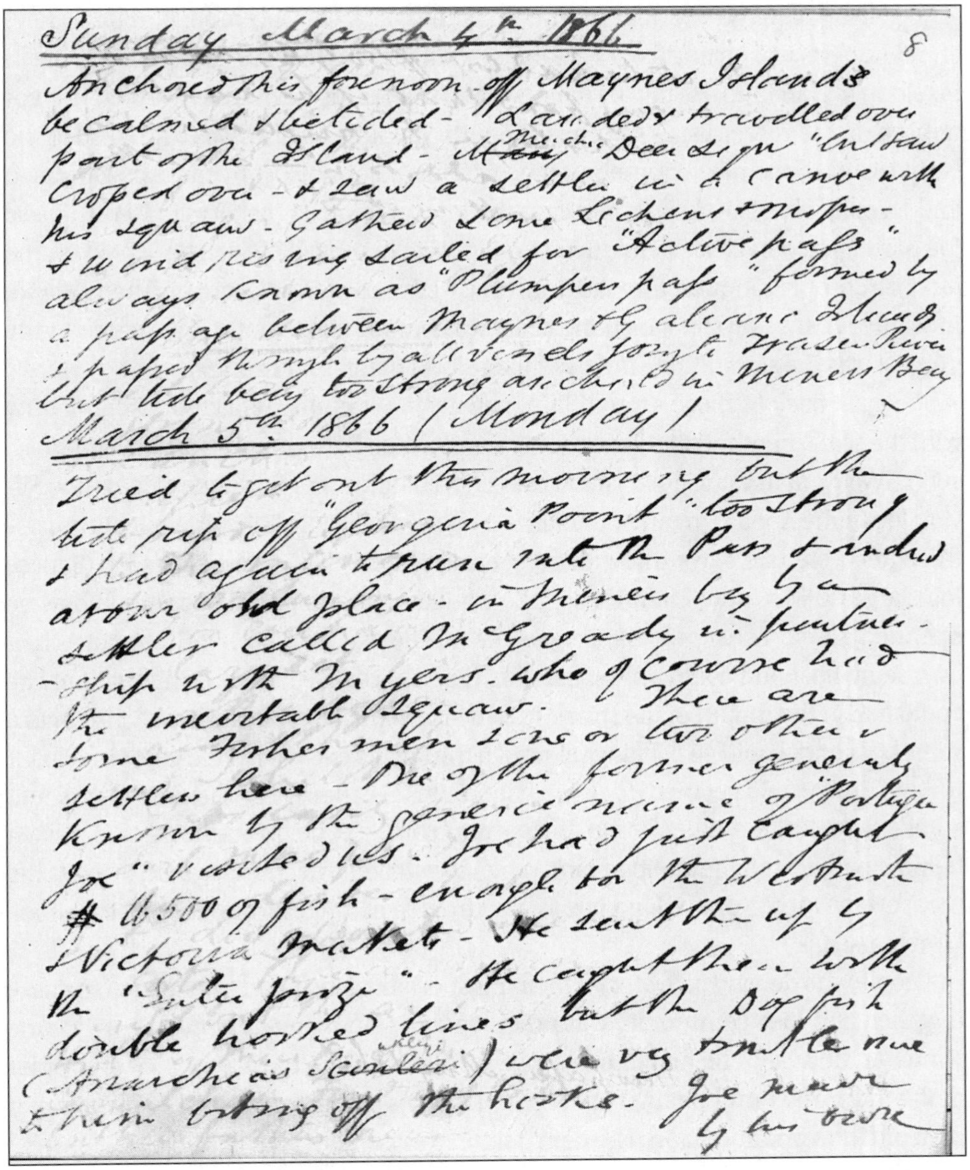

Sunday March 4th 1866 8
Anchored this forenoon off Maynes Islands
becalmed & ticided - Landed & travelled over
part of the Island - Micheli Deer sign "..."
Cropped over - & saw a settler in a canoe with
his squaw - Gathered some Lichens & Mosses -
& wind rising sailed for "Active pass"
always known as "Plumper pass" formed by
a passage between Maynes & Galiano Island
& passed through by all vessels going to Fraser River
but tide being too strong anchored in Miners Bay
March 5th 1866 (Monday)

Tried to get out this morning but the
tide rip off "Georgina Point" too strong
& had again to run into the Pass & indeed
at our old place - in Miners bay by a
settler called McGready in partner-
-ship with Myers. who of course had
the inevitable squaw. There are
some Fishermen here or two other
settlers here - One of the former generally
known by the generic name of "Portuguese
Joe" visited us. Joe had just caught
lb 500 of fish - enough for the Westminster
Victoria markets - He sent them up by
the "Enterprize" - He caught them with
double hooked lines but the Dog fish
(Acanthias Sucklii) were very troublesome
them biting off the hooks. Joe made
by his own

Reverend Roberts' journal gives insight into the lives of Portuguese Joe and others living in the Reid Island area. Here he describes how Joe caught enough fish "for the Westminster and Victoria markets." BC Archives MS794

Whenwhutston & Charlie Seeyakahail witnessed the note." Three years later, on April 16, 1885, Roberts described how he went with "Indian Joe & Tom to Penelakut to see Charlie Quiem who appears to be dying. I wrote Some letters for him about monies due to him [by] Joe Silvia & Geo. Whenwhutston witnessed 'his mark.' Silvia gave him a dose of Castor oil." Quiem's widow pursued the debt. Roberts wrote on May 7, 1887: "Mrs. Quiem & her 2 daughters (Sarah & the one married to the Comox Indian) & son in law came to see me about monies due to her by Curran & Portuguese Joe Silvia."

As Reverend Roberts' diaries attest, Portuguese Joe was always out to make the best deal, which was not necessarily in others' interests. A family member has reflected that "he was a bit of a rascal with the Indians," and "it was Lucy who kept him alive." She was the connection with Native people who secured the family's well-being. "Granny saved his hide. Except for Granny, they would have shot and ate him."

Joe Silvey acquired a certain stature along the coast. On December 8, 1882, as Reverend Roberts was sailing from Nanaimo to Kuper: "We met Portuguese Joe going in his sloop to Nanaimo. He told us that the wind was strong below the Narrows." Joe got himself on the voters' list as soon as the South Nanaimo District was organized in the early 1890s. In the next enumeration he was joined on the list by his sons Domingo and Joseph, who, like their father, gave their occupation as "fisherman." Portuguese Joe participated in civic life in other ways as well. In the fall of 1888 he served on the jury of a coroner's inquest into the death of a Native named Solesum on Thetis Island. Indicative of the ways in which the coast was bound together, the interpreter at the inquest was the stepmother-in-law of Joe's eldest daughter Elizabeth.

Joe gave back to those around him, usually in ways that reflected his familiarity with the sea. Sometimes his generosity was informal. Roberts noted on November 14, 1886: "We went as far as Reid Island & anchored in front of Portuguese Joe's (Joe Silvia). Joe Came Aboard for an hour or so—he gave us a Codfish & some salt herrings—the latter were bad & we threw them overboard next day." Other times Portuguese Joe's largesse was more intentional. Joe's granddaughter Irene has described how he operated a food fishery for the Penelakuts of Kuper Island, who did not have their own seine boat and could only spear fish. "Portuguese Joe had a permit that only he could fish in the mouth of the river with a beach seine. Every year Grandfather had a seine boat and would go fish dog salmon in the fall; he got a permit to get food fish for Indians, and would get them for them. He would take them over and then they would smoke them for the winter." As to the reason: "Portugee [her pronunciation] Joe liked helping people and they helped him. When they killed a deer they would bring some meat over. A lot of Kuper Island people had trouble getting fish and Portugee Joe took it on himself."

People who depend on water for their transportation and livelihood tend to socialize together, and Joe's community was no exception. Fishing boats would tie up for the winter at Mud Bay. The first one to arrive set down next to the wharf and stuck poles in the mud. The next boat tied up next to the poles and planted more poles, another boat did the same and so on. The men "would winter there talking with Grandpa Joe." Among the winter sojourners and also throughout the year, there were "lots of Portuguese people who came around Reid." According to Irene, "Grandpa used to be the leader of them."

Visits from long-time friends such as Peter Smith of the old whaling days must have confirmed for Portuguese Joe the wisdom of having got his own island. He likely reflected on the freedom it gave his family to make their lives on their own terms. In 1887 the new city of Vancouver, brought into being by the completion of the transcontinental railroad, successfully lobbied the Dominion government for access to the government reserve, including Brockton Point. Stanley Park, as it was named, became the recreational preserve of newcomers from Canada and Britain who wanted it to reflect their mix of values and priorities. It was almost inevitable that long-time residents, including members of the Smith, Gonsalves and Baker families, would eventually be forced out of their homes. The simmering dispute, which reached its climax in the mid-1920s, reminded the Silvey family how right they had been to leave Brockton Point, although they likely did not realize the full extent to which persons like themselves were being marginalized in the new British Columbia.

On Reid Island, the Silveys were left far more to their own devices. They lived closer to the frontier according to both aboriginal and newcomer ways. In many respects Joe Silvey remained a Portuguese peasant all his life. Just as his father had done for him on Pico Island, Portuguese Joe was determined to imbue his children with traditional values along with the ability to make a living. They learned an appreciation of their Portuguese identity, which they would carry with them proudly through their own and their descendants' lifetimes. Khaltinaht had instilled aboriginal values in her children, and Lucy attempted to do much the same with hers. The family was multilingual. As a matter of course they spoke Portuguese, the trading jargon of Chinook, the local Cowichan language, and English.

Formal education was another matter. It had not been part of Joe's upbringing and did not acquire much value. Elizabeth, who had not attended school as a child, recalled how "Father had a man at Reid Island, he boarded with us for six months, and that is all the education I got; I can read a little." At the time of the 1891 census, the two oldest children still at home, Domingo and Mary, were recorded

Reverend Robert James Roberts and his wife on Kuper Island. Despite his initial misgivings, Roberts married Elizabeth and James Walker. BC Archives D05957

as able to read but not to write, whereas Joe, age 12, John, who was nine, and Antonio, age seven, could do neither. In 1901 Tony was described as literate, but not so Manuel, age 15, Henry, age 11, or Lena, who was six. Schooling was not a high priority.

Joe Silvey's sons in particular received an education in the life of the sea. From their early teens they went fishing with him. Elizabeth recalled a herring seine licence "made out to Silvey & sons." A grandson who knew Portuguese Joe as a young child and who had been named for him took pride all his life in how "they fished as they had fished in Portugal; making their own nets in the winter and, during the fishing season, taking the nets out into deep water surrounding the fish and then dragging the net ashore." A dozen men were needed to do so. Even though Portuguese Joe had retreated, so he thought, from "civilization," it eventually caught up with him, according to a grandson. "Around the close of the century, beach seine licence fees of $10 were imposed. Old Joe Silvey refused to pay. The next season his net was seized and burned at Nanaimo."

Joe taught his sons not only how to make a living, but to take care while doing so. Sealing schooners were among the vessels that tied up for the winter at Reid Island,

Above: Manuel Silvey with a group of fishermen and sealers in front of the Commercial Hotel, Steveston, 1890s. Left to right: unknown man with bicycle, Manuel Silvey, Fred Corkill, Jesse Plant, the hotel-keeper, Frank Davis, Alexander King and Arthur Willie Palua (both lost in the *Triumph* in 1903), and Bill Shepard. Courtesy the Fisherman Publishing Society, UBC Special Collections

Opposite top: Portuguese Joe's daughter Josephine had eight children by the time she was 30. Courtesy Rocky Sampson

Opposite bottom: Joe's oldest son Domingo and his wife Josephine standing in front of the house Joe built on Reid Island. Courtesy Chris Thompson

and it may have been this proximity that encouraged Tony, when he was just 15, to sign up with the *Triumph*, reputed to be the largest and fastest sailing ship in the Victoria sealing fleet. Sealing was a lucrative activity that required trips north to the Bering Sea of six or more months' duration. His father considered Tony "far too young" and bought out his contract. "Dad went to sign up on a sealer and Grandfather got him off." He may have saved Tony's life—the *Triumph* sank four years later, in 1903, with all 35 men lost.

As time passed, Portuguese Joe's older daughters went their own ways. Joe's goal for them was very much that which had befallen Elizabeth. He wanted them to become good wives and mothers within a long tradition of peasant families. Josephine, Joe's second child by Khaltinaht, was a mother at age 16. By the time she was 30, she had eight children with her husband, a Ladysmith storekeeper. Following his death, Josephine found another husband, a Chemainus logger of Scottish descent, born in rural Ontario. Steve Anderson was 10 years her senior, and in 1901 he earned a very respectable $900.

Portuguese Joe's third daughter Mary, born at Brockton Point about six years after Josephine's birth on nearby Pasley Island, followed a similar path. Mary was still in her teens when she married David Roberts, a Welsh widower more than twice her age. Roberts had four motherless sons and a farm that needed tending on nearby Gabriola Island. Whatever happened to the relationship, by 1901 Mary, age 24, had four children and, like her sister Josephine, she was living with a rural Ontarian of Scots descent 10 years older than she was—a logger named Richard Brown. Joe Silvey's three eldest daughters were caught in a timeless pattern of female domesticity.

There was much less pressure on Joe Silvey's sons to settle down young. As males they possessed far more freedom of action than did their sisters. When they married, they were expected to be able to support both themselves and their families. It took time to acquire the means, hence the acceptability of a significant age difference within a marriage. According to grandchildren, with their "big long handlebars" and gleaming black hair, the Silvey sons were considered "catches." They had little difficulty finding mates as soon as they were in a position to do so.

Joe's eldest son Domingo had his first child by Josephine Crocker, five years his junior, when he was 23 years old. Her family lived just across the water at Chemainus. Her father Simeon Crocker, who like so many others combined logging and fishing, had come from Maine. Her mother Pakaltinatt, or Lucy, was from Kuper Island. Joseph was born in 1897 on Reid Island. John, known as Jack, followed two years later. Whereas Joseph's birth went unrecorded, Domingo had the Catholic priest on nearby Kuper register John for him on the grounds that he "cannot write." Like his father, Domingo preferred the life of a fisherman. He also did whatever was necessary to support his young family, which included working as a logger from time to time.

Domingo stayed close to home, as was expected of the eldest son, but his brother Joseph struck out on his own. In 1901 young Joe was working in Chemainus as a longshoreman, loading vessels come to pick up lumber. It was hard work, for which he earned an impressive $900 in a year. On June 2, 1900, the Catholic priest went over to Chemainus from Kuper Island to marry Joseph to Maria King. She was the daughter of an early Greek settler on Salt Spring Island, who had anglicized his name and married a Saanich woman named Mary Tegurviei. Like young Joe, Maria had grown up in a fishing family, but one that was star-crossed—two of her three brothers perished in the *Triumph* disaster.

The second generation of Silveys was fast finding its way. By the turn of the century Portuguese Joe's two daughters by Khaltinaht, Elizabeth and Josephine, had produced well over a dozen children between them. Lucy's two oldest, Domingo and Mary, were the parents of another six. Young Joe was newly married. Joe and Lucy's five other children, John, Tony, Manuel, Henry and Lena, ranged in age from five to 16.

No More Adventures

Portuguese Joe took special pleasure in his acquisition of Reid Island as a secure home for his family. As a young man, his son Tony drove oxen used for logging on Vancouver Island, and when he came home for the weekend, he told his father excitedly about an opportunity to buy much of the area around Saltair north of Chemainus. Joe advised him against doing so, for "we have the island, we don't need it." The island was a haven for the family, especially in view of the many changes that occurred during his lifetime. Joe's namesake grandson, born in 1897, recalled being taken across to Chemainus in a rowboat: "I remember my grandfather when I was just a young boy, my grandfather calling in great excitement, 'Come and look, there is a boat going

Portuguese Joe's son Tony
stayed on Reid Island.
Courtesy Jessica Casey

by with no sails and no oars,' and that was the very first gas boat I ever saw." One of Portuguese Joe's favourite expressions was: "Well, I'll be damned," and this time he expressed a very loud, "Well, I'll be damned, what's that?!"

Portuguese Joe was a tough man who was never sick. But in the fall of 1900 he caught a chill while "fishing for salmon with a net." According to his eldest daughter Elizabeth, he was "living in an old shack at Chemainus" and "had some men working with him, but he went home to Reid Island." Elizabeth, who lived not far away, decided that she wanted to see him, although she had not been told he was sick. "I was living at Ladysmith; three miles toward Nanaimo; right on the highway; on a little farm; that was where all my [10] children were raised." She shared her premonition with her sons. "I don't know what's the matter with me. I want to go see Grandpa. I've been thinking about him all night. I can't sleep." Elizabeth and one of her sons set out. "We got a little rowboat. It is only 10 miles from Ladysmith to Reid Island, and we rowed over. And then when we got there, there was my father still sick. He was sitting up in a chair and looked so ill. He said to me, 'My dear Elizabeth; Papa's so sick, I'll tell you later.' Later he told me he could not make water." The next morning Joe was put "in one of the sailboats he had just built." His daughter got hold of her husband "working right on the bay getting out some timber," and they took him to a doctor.

Joe recovered, but a year later he suffered a second attack, and this time it was fatal. On his death on January 17, 1902, on Reid Island, likely in his mid-70s, he was described as a fisherman. "Father is buried on Reid Island; that was his wish. He is buried on his own property."

Portuguese Joe's most precious asset was Reid Island, but whatever wishes he might have had for its future, he left no will. Domingo's status

Portuguese Joe and Lucy were laid to rest in the small family cemetery on Reid Island.
Courtesy Rocky Sampson

as the eldest son determined that he would take charge, but the situation soon grew messy. Portuguese Joe had not turned Lot 35 into a Crown grant. It could not be distributed among his widow and 10 children until outright ownership was secured, for which $400 in costs and taxes had to be paid. Domingo managed to get Crown grants for the smaller Lots 34 and 36 he had preempted, but not for Lot 35, which was sold for unpaid taxes at the end of 1919. Domingo used the opportunity to purchase it outright and on that basis secure a mortgage to cover the cost, thereby saving his father's legacy of Reid Island, but to the advantage of his own family.

Portuguese Joe's widow Lucy was in her mid-40s at the time of his death. Her youngest child Lena was just seven. Lucy continued to live in the family house and during the summer brought in a bit of money by making nets on the Fraser River. As she sought to make a new life for herself, she found companionship with an Irishman named Joe Watson, whom she met when he was cooking on a seine boat for her son Tony. A granddaughter remembered Lucy as "an old granny, just like grannies used to be, sitting in a rocking chair, teaching us how to shell peas, peel an apple, make bread." Lucy died on Reid Island on August 13, 1934. A measure of the self-sufficiency that characterized Reid Islanders can be seen on her death certificate. Under the category "Undertaker" is written: "By relatives."

Dozens of family members and friends turned out for Lucy Kwahama Kwatleematt's funeral. In the front row (from left to right) are Elizabeth Silvey, Clara Silvey Bell, Edith Beale holding hands with her mother Lena Silvey Beale, Lucy's second husband Joe Watson, Henry Silvey, Tony Silvey and Alice Aleck Silvey.
Courtesy Jessica Casey

Lucy outlived Joe by more than 30 years, and saw how their family expanded both on and off Reid Island.
Courtesy Jessica Casey

Continuing Portuguese Joe's Story

The remarkable adventures of Portuguese Joe Silvey did not end with his death in 1902, or even that of his second wife Lucy a third of a century later. He instilled in each of his 10 children ways of seeing and doing that they carried with them through their lifetimes. The means by which the Silvey sons and daughters dealt with the legacy their parents bequeathed them are part of Portuguese Joe's story.

The young Silveys continued to follow in their father's footsteps in their choice of occupation, and they looked to the example of their parents' neighbours and acquaintances when it came time to start a family. The sons fished and logged, much as Portuguese Joe had done. They chose wives whose priority was home and hearth, just as it was for their sisters. Through the First World War, British Columbia's newcomer population consisted of two to three times as many men as women. A daughter of mixed heritage could choose between a newcomer of modest means, as had Josephine and Mary, and another person of mixed race, as had happened to Elizabeth. Either way, women were expected to submerge their identities into those of their husbands, making a hybrid daughter-in-law just tolerable. In sharp contrast, no newcomer family wanted, under any circumstances, a mixed-race son-in-law. A son's choice was between another hybrid person like himself, as Domingo and Joe had done, or an aboriginal woman. All of Portuguese Joe's children believed that they were exercising free will when they settled down, but their decisions also reflected both their father's desires for them and the larger social pressures at work in British Columbia.

Khaltinaht's Daughters

Upon Portuguese Joe's death, his two families divided. His daughters by Khaltinaht went their own ways, and Elizabeth never returned to live on Reid Island. At about the end of the First World War, she left the husband she had married so reluctantly and by whom she had had 10 children in rapid succession. "I was just his 'slave,'" Elizabeth asserted two decades later. Jimmy Walker lived for a time with family members in a coastal logging camp, where his great-granddaughter Marie recalled, he used to "tease us with the old Native words." As for Elizabeth, whom she saw from time to time, "she always wore long black skirts and was stately and stern." In 1938 Elizabeth was living on relief in "an old dilapidated rooming house" at 721 Cambie Street in Vancouver. Vancouver City Archivist Major J.S. Matthews visited Elizabeth in what he described as "her solitary room, at the back, about 10 by 12 feet square, and containing a poor bed, two chairs, a gas cooking plate and a small tan heating stove."

Elizabeth continued to take pride in her mother Khaltinaht's family and, in her later years, attempted to renew relationships with the Musqueam and Squamish people. By this time aboriginal people had internalized their forced separation from the dominant society in profound ways. "I did apply once to be allowed to share in the distribution of Indian monies," Elizabeth said, "and there was a meeting over at Capilano Creek, and I might have got my share, but Old Mary Capilano, [Chief] Capilano Joe's wife, objected, and said something sneering about the women who went off and became white, and gave themselves airs."

In 1939 Elizabeth took a chance and attended a potlatch on the Musqueam Reserve south of Vancouver, reminiscent of the one she had attended with her mother at Whoi Whoi two-thirds of a century earlier. No sooner had she sat down than the son of her mother's cousin recognized her and invited her to the head table. Informally he gave her much the same message as she had got on the Capilano Reserve. "If I had not become a white woman I would have had a home and land. I would have had a home and land, if I had stayed Indian, and I did not know how high up in [status in] Indian life I was." At the same time he publicly defended Elizabeth's presence. "John [Guerin] got up to make a speech, and he spoke in Indian, but I knew what he was saying. I don't think he knew I did. He told all those Indians there not to insult me, that I was a great-granddaughter of Old Chief Kiapilano."

Elizabeth remained close to her cousin Christine, daughter of her mother's sister Rowia and Navvy Jack Thomas. After she was informally recognized at Musqueam, Elizabeth accepted an invitation via Christine to visit Gassy Jack Deighton's widow Madeleine, a basket maker on the Mission Reserve in North Vancouver. "She says she remembers me when I was a little girl, and Father lived at one end of the Gastown beach and Gassy Jack at the other." The visit was

a success. Elizabeth discovered, to her great pleasure, that "she knew my father, Joe Silvey, 'Portuguese Joe,' and she knew me when I was little." Joe Silvey's eldest daughter died in Vancouver on July 14, 1945, at the age of 78.

Elizabeth's sister Josephine spent most of her adult life along the coast. She cooked in logging camps, near where her husband Steve Anderson logged and fished. Josephine "had never gone to school and couldn't read," her great-grandchild Florence explained, "so she had to do all her cooking from memory." As soon as the children grew up, they mostly headed off to "the big city," but Josephine and her husband liked the outdoor life and held on as long as they could. Eventually age and poor health caught up with them. Josephine died in Vancouver on March 27, 1930.

Perhaps because Josephine did not have the opportunity to know her mother, she identified herself as Portuguese—so strongly that her daughter, who gave the information on Josephine's death registration, recorded only that part of her mother's heritage. She was so convinced of it that she reported Josephine's mother Khaltinaht, as well as her father Portuguese Joe, had been born in Portugal.

Sons on Reid Island

In accordance with Portuguese tradition, Joe Silvey's eldest son Domingo took seriously his responsibility as the keeper of Reid Island. On December 20, 1905, he formally wed the mother of his children, Josephine Crocker, after being prodded to do so by the priest on nearby Kuper Island. In the story passed down through their children, the priest admonished them: "You get married or else." Families of similar background were closely linked: Josephine's brother Abraham married Louisa Silva, a daughter of Portuguese Joe's countryman, and they settled down near the Silva clan on Gabriola Island.

Domingo, Josephine and their seven children lived at the eastern edge of the small "egg" on Mud Bay. Everyday life was self-sustaining, as far as possible. Domingo's

Domingo formally married Josephine Crocker after being coerced by a Catholic priest on nearby Kuper Island. The two had previously "eloped" and were married in a native ceremony on the banks of the Chemainus River.

oldest son Joe, born in 1897, recalled: "When I was young we had fish, vegetables were grown on north Galiano, we would trade fish for vegetables. The only things we needed cash for were tobacco, salt, sugar and gasoline." Josephine played a major role. "Mother could do things," Joe said. "She would see the recipe and it would stick in her mind." She crocheted, which had the practical benefit of keeping "her fingers nimble, and it helped her to mend nets." Domingo likely made her large net-mending needles. The family served as a centre for community on Reid Island. "We were really at-home people, and if someone didn't have a place we would put them on the verandah or where-have-you. I think in those days people were more considerate."

According to a niece who grew up on Reid Island, Domingo was "into everything"—troller, seiner, logger, drag seiner. He also acquired a reputation as "a very good boat builder." Young Joe once mused how, "in those early days, times were hard and men were tough; they had to be to survive." The family possessed at least one visible reminder of tradition, a big black pot "the size of a dining table and as high." Portuguese Joe had used it, and Domingo after him. "You put dogfish livers in it to get out the oil, you could smell it, it smelled like 'heaven,' we said, by which we meant 'hell.'" One of Domingo's daughters recalled how "we went to Vancouver and you could smell us, we went to the theatre in Vancouver and people moved away from us."

Domingo followed his father's example in mentoring his sons in the life of the sea at an early age. His eldest son Joe recalled: "I went fishing with him. At this time I was between nine and 10 years old. I was big enough to pull some of the fish in and I did what I could. I didn't make the nets at this age but I made them after I got about 15 or 16 years of age. I could make any kind of net." Domingo and his sons fished and logged on much of the Gulf Islands and part of Vancouver Island. "We would camp on Galiano, we moved off of Reid to the gulf side of Galiano." Silvey's Cove, as the site on the northeastern shore of Galiano became known, is still considered a prime location for landing boats. Domingo used horses and a steam donkey to bring out logs to be sold to the coal mines around Nanaimo and for wood-burning tugboats.

The one activity that did not much tempt second-generation Silveys was whaling. A spurt of new interest in the industry rose briefly in the early 20th century. Domingo's

Dressing up and going to town was an exciting but sometimes difficult experience for the Silveys, who were used to a more frontier-style existence. Pictured here is Nellie Francis (Anderson) MacDonald, one of Portuguese Joe's granddaughters, and her friend Barbara May Kimball. Courtesy Rocky Sampson

son Joe described how, when he was a boy, "we would sit there and watch the whalers" chase down "whales in front of our house on Reid Island." Young Joe did not quite understand what was happening until, travelling the north shore of Valdes Island with his father, they came upon "a whale lying on its back with 13 to 14 Japanese working on it." Joe was perplexed. "I asked the old man and he said, 'That is a whale, don't you know? You see them in front of the house all the time.' I said, 'I've never seen them like that.'" Domingo explained to young Joe that his grandfather, Portuguese Joe, had been a whaler, making $1.25 to $1.50 per four-gallon can of oil for use in coal miners' pit lights.

A neighbour was determined to get in on the action and, convinced that by definition "a Silvey is a whaler," he persuaded Domingo's younger brothers Tony and Manuel to accompany him. According to Domingo's son Joe, the trip was a disaster. "The whale was sleeping in the water and they got too close to the whale and the whale tipped the boat." Tony was scared off, but Manuel talked their older brother Joe into having a try. "Joe went out as brave as could be, so they harpooned a whale, they managed to get the harpoon on him and he took off for Dodds Narrows. They got the rope and tied her down and they all laid down in the bottom of the boat and every once in a while, they would peek over the side. The boat was making one mile an hour and the whale was doing 15. Every once in a while he would pop up and get his wind and then down he would go again." Finally, in desperation, they "cut the rope and away went the whale." To save face on returning home, the story goes, they "said the whale bit the line off." There were no more whaling adventures.

Theirs was a demanding but satisfying way of life, which was disrupted by World War I. As far as everyone knew, Domingo's two oldest sons Joe and Jack were "working on Galiano logging." According to a younger sister, "Joe went to town and came back in a uniform— we all got sick with it." Jack did the same. "Because Joe joined up, Jack had

Right: One of Domingo's boats. Domingo developed a reputation as "a very good boat builder."
Courtesy Eunice Weatherell

Opposite top: In 1917, Domingo's oldest son Joe sneaked off and joined the armed forces.
Courtesy Chris Thompson

Opposite bottom: Like his older brother, Jack signed up to join the war effort, but his father refused to let him go overseas and he was discharged—a humiliating experience he never forgot.
Courtesy Chris Thompson

to, he would do whatever Joe did." Their official applications to join the Canadian Over-Seas Expeditionary Force are both dated June 8, 1917. Twenty-year-old Joe and 18-year-old Jack gave their occupations as loggers. Joe described himself as 5'9" with black hair, brown eyes and "dark" complexion, Jack as 5'6" with black hair, brown eyes and "red" complexion. Both boys were conscious that they were not "fair," the usual response to the last question.

Domingo, who was ill at the time, could not bear to lose both his sons. He openly opposed them to try to get at least one of them out. Jack's application bears the notation: "Discharged, 23-6-17. D.S." Domingo's second son was humiliated. "I don't think he ever forgave Pa," his siblings recalled. Joe spent two years in military service: "I was overseas 18 or 19 months." He spent time in the trenches and got gassed. "We did a lot of praying in those days," a sister remembered. The prayers had the desired effect. Joe returned and, after a stint long-shoring in Chemainus for 80¢ an hour plus board, he settled down on the northern tip of the big egg. His younger brother Jack lived on the southern tip of the small egg.

Both Joe and Jack married women from among coastal and island mixed-race fishing families. Joe's wife Amelia Wilson was part of a formidable Fraser River clan that, on being forced off the Coquitlam Indian Reserve, settled at Canoe Pass near present-day Ladner. They met on the Skeena River, where both Joe and Amelia's family were fishing. Jack's wife Laura was a granddaughter of James McFadden, a Hudson's Bay fur trader, and of a Bella Bella woman, and of Edwin Rosman, a Cornishman come with the gold rush, and his Tlingit wife. Laura grew up at Fernwood on northeast Salt Spring Island, where her father, like so many others of similar mixed background, made a living as a sealer. The story goes that the couple met when Jack rowed over to see the medical doctor on Salt Spring. Laura was about to go on a mail run and offered to give him a ride from the Fernwood dock in her horse and buggy.

Portugueses Joe's son John, eight years Domingo's junior, also used Reid Island as a base. Like the other Silvey men, Jack married a woman from the neighbourhood. Charlotte Peterson was born on Gabriola to a Danish farmer and a Native woman named Jane, recalled as "strong and strict." Jack and a partner had a logging and log-salvaging business at Yellow Point north of Chemainus. On October 8, 1907, Jack was murdered while on his way home to Reid Island by rowboat. According to one version of events passed down through time, "John was shot while on the boat; he was buying clams and it was known he had a lot of money, so he was shot and robbed." A variation of the story, also told in the family, has him heading to Reid with $50 he had received in

Right: John Laurence Silvey married Laura Georgina McFadden on February 26th, 1922, at Saint Mark's church, Salt Spring Island.
Courtesy Eunice Weatherell

Opposite top: Jack's daughter Eunice Silvey relaxing on Reid Island. One of the salteries is visible behind her.
Courtesy Eunice Weatherell

Opposite bottom: Although he was disinherited by the actions of his older brother Domingo, Portuguese Joe's fourth son Tony remained on Reid Island out of affection for his mother Lucy Kwatleematt.
Courtesy Rocky Sampson

Nanaimo for "a big raft of logs." Everyone had their suspicions as to who was responsible, but no one ever knew for sure.

Portuguese Joe's fourth son Tony, who was born in 1884, two years after John, also stayed on Reid Island. He settled on its western edge despite his very deep unhappiness over being disinherited. In 1923 he, his mother and seven siblings initiated legal proceedings on the grounds that Lot 35 could not have legally been sold for taxes when "the title was still in the name of the Crown." Land records in the British Columbia Archives indicate provincial authorities were aware of a lack of due process, but at the same time unwilling to reverse the sale. Domingo retained ownership of Lot 35, much to his siblings' dismay. Tony is said to have remained on Reid out of affection for his mother.

On September 29, 1904, Tony wed Philomena Beale, the 18-year-old daughter of an American farmer on Galiano and a Penelakut woman whose father was a chief on Kuper Island, but the marriage did not last. In one version of the story, Minnie asked her husband to let her go home for a visit. Tony asked her to wait a day while he went fishing. "He came home and she was gone, he couldn't write and couldn't look for her." Not only had Minnie gone back to her family, she took their infant son Thomas with her. In another telling of the same event, "Philomena ran off with Jimmy Crocker from Gabriola." Indicative of the ties that bound together coastal families of mixed race, Jimmy was Domingo Silvey's brother-in-law.

After his wife's bunk, Tony turned to a Kuper Island woman, Alice Aleck, or Swealt. According to their daughter Irene, Alice's Cowichan name, which means "little tiny thing," was given to her because she was only "four feet and a bit" tall. Alice's parents had drowned when she was just eight months old and her brother Dave, or Thaamalt, was a couple of years older. Their maternal aunt took them in and, when they reached school age, sent them to the Kuper Island residential school run by the Oblates, where they remained into young adulthood.

Alice was aged six when she entered the Kuper Island school on November 20, 1898, just over a year after her brother David had arrived there. The school's 60-some pupils were closely monitored, being allowed just two visits home a year: three weeks in June or July and a few days over Christmas.

As was the usual practice in residential schools, pupils were taught a combination of basic literacy and practical skills. According to records held in the British Columbia Archives, the term after Alice arrived, the 28 girls made 27 dresses, 23 aprons,

Tony's great love Alice Aleck entered the Kuper Island residential school when she was just six.
BC Archives PDP 05505

16 napkins, 10 yards of lace, 2 pairs of pants, 2 chemises, 1 big curtain and 2 mattress ticks. Alice gradually advanced from "sewing & darning" to "machine sewing" by 1906. While no conduct book survives for the girls, it does for the boys. Their punishments for misbehaviour during the years Alice was enrolled ranged from "confinement, writing lines, bread and water" to private or public "reprimands." Throughout her life, Alice appreciated the lessons in everyday living she learned at Kuper Island. Her daughter Rose said that Alice "could sew just like a seamstress."

Tony Silvey and Alice Aleck may have met through Domingo's wife Josephine. Her brothers Abe and Jimmy—who was implicated in the departure of Tony's wife—both attended the Kuper Island school at the same time as Alice. The sanctions that the Catholic Church put on human relations had their effect on the couple: however great their commitment to each other, Antonio Silvey remained in the eyes of the church bigamously married to the errant Philomena. The church did not permit divorce, regardless of the circumstances. Tony's former wife clearly suffered as well. In 1917, using her maiden name and describing herself as a spinster, Minnie Beale married James Crocker in Anglican Christ Church Cathedral in Victoria. They described themselves as living in Crofton, where Jimmy was a logger.

In 1935 Alice died of tuberculosis, leaving Tony with a houseful of children, the youngest only five months old. "The fine way in which he raised his young family by himself won the admiration of all who knew him," Tony's obituary stated. He brought them up much as he himself was raised. "I didn't know how to speak English for a long time. I got the Chinook mixed up with the Portuguese. Dad spoke Portuguese. He threw Chinook at us. All of the old people knew the Cowichan language, even some of the white fishermen. So, for a long time we didn't know there were different nationalities. We thought everyone was the same." Tony's daughter Irene astutely reflected that "they were a smart bunch of people, they could speak all those languages."

Reid Island also had a couple of tenants. A well-connected Englishman recalled only as Percy "needed a place to stay." When he and young Joe were in the trenches together, he told Joe that his wife had left him and he wanted to escape "to the colonies." Joe invited George Percy Blizard home with him. He explained how he helped Percy build a small cabin on the edge of his holding, and there this self-described "distant relative of Winston Churchill" settled down. Percy's family sent him regular remittances, perhaps to ensure that he stayed away.

Percy's elite education at Westminster Public School in London seemed a lifetime away. He brought his wife's clothes with him from England and sometimes wore them. His eccentricities were for the most part accommodated. Grandchildren raised on Reid Island remember how "he wore his wife's clothes all the time," that is, unless he was around his own place, where he "never wore clothes and so we had to whistle that we were coming." Sometimes he decorated his nude body with a sash. Once, when he was going to Ladysmith with the Silveys in their boat, "he came down wearing his wife's silk stockings, skirt, white blouse, high heels, little hat." That was too much. "Cousin Jack made him go back and put on jeans." Gradually Percy became more peculiar. "He was out of his head by the time he left, the police came to get him, he said he had to go back, he dug up a box of old remittance cheques, none of them had been cashed." Portuguese Joe's grandchildren emphasized that Percy was

Although life at the residential school was restrictive, Alice (front row, far left) always appreciated the practical skills she developed there.
Courtesy Rocky Sampson

George Percy Blizard, an English friend of Joe's from the war, settled in this cabin on Reid Island, where his eccentricities were largely accepted. *Courtesy Rocky Sampson*

not unique but typical of a whole number of individuals who during these years were able to make a life on their own terms on an island.

On the west side of Reid, near where Tony lived, two Japanese families had got permission to erect wharves and construct herring salteries. They went into operation in about 1908, and soon numerous others sprang up on nearby islands, including Valdes and Galiano. The Tanakas and the Kashos lived all year-round in houses just above the Reid Island salteries. Tony's daughter Irene recalled them as elderly couples without children of their own. "They started in October/November to seine the herring," she explained. Two boats with a net between them would purse it tight as soon as it filled with herring. The seiners would unload the herring onto scows, from which the fish would go on a conveyer to the salteries, which was set on piles at the edge of the water. The herring was put into vats in layers, which Irene remembered as being five feet deep, 30 feet wide, and 16 feet (1.5 x 9 x 5 metres) long. The fish was not heated, just salted—"layer of salt, layer of herring, layer of salt, and so forth." Portuguese Joe used a similar process at Brockton Point.

The two salteries required much labour on short notice. Domingo's son Joe described upwards of a hundred Japanese float homes in the area. Each saltery required about 150 workers during the height of the season. "When the herring was coming, they would start a fire and the Indians would paddle over." Tony Silvey worked as net boss, in charge of making nets. Perhaps for that reason, his daughter Rose explained, the Japanese "watchmen used to bring us cake and cookies and canned pineapple."

Tony's daughter Irene washed dishes at the salteries when she was 12 and 13 years old. There were separate cookhouses for the different groups of workers. "The old Japanese women would ring the bell," she recalled, "and I would run down the little trail from our house and wash the dishes, there were only bowls and chopsticks at the Japanese cookhouse, so I liked it much more than the white cookhouse, where there were cups and saucers and everything else." The salted herring was shipped to Japan. The annual round continued until the Second World War, when the two families were evacuated, along with others of Japanese descent living on the coast, and the salteries perforce abandoned.

Through the recollections of Domingo's and Tony's children, it is possible to glimpse everyday life on Reid Island during their childhoods in the 1930s, when the Great Depression raged. Third-generation Silveys contributed to the family economy in many ways, including washing dishes at the salteries and digging clams. "We gave all our money to our dad," said Irene, and sometimes "Dad would buy us a chocolate bar and we would divide it into pieces."

Men on relief got $29 per month. "Father worked on the road to get it. We were so ashamed that we had to say Father was away, not that we were on relief and he was working on the road." Tony's daughter Irene recalled "eating cabbage and stuff when times were tough in the winter." Their father would tell them that this was food "fit for a king." They thought he was referring to the king of England but it was to himself, since he was known as the "king of the cod fishermen" and had the nickname "King." Sometimes it was outsiders who came to the rescue. According to Irene, a good sa-

Two Japanese families—the Tanakas and the Kashos—built herring salteries on the west side of Reid Island. At their peak, the salteries employed about 150 workers each. Courtesy Eunice Weatherell

maritan of sorts went "up and down the coast in a boat, he would steal from the various logging camps and then repaint the boat." One side would be painted white and the other green, so that when he went back down the coast no one would realize it was the same boat. "He would give poor people what he stole…He unloaded at the rock [a flat rock on Reid Island]—three cases of bully beef, canned goods—he left it for us."

Everyone banded together. "It was a good life—we helped each other." Food was got where and when it could be had. "When potatoes were for sale, we would get enough for all the family." Barter was the rule. "We wouldn't sell anything, we would pick crabapples, everything was traded. We had mush, eggs, our own bacon and ham. We made our own lard and soap. We had our own blueberry patch, we had our own little horn lake (so named because there was a horn on a tree near it), we had our own playing field, we had everything on that island, it was a happy time."

"We were like one big family on the island." The isolation of Reid Island allowed the Silveys and others to maintain a Portuguese lifestyle that in retrospect acquired an idyllic quality. Third- and fourth-generation Silveys who grew up there have similar memories of their childhoods. "We were happy, we were content, we had love. There was togetherness in those days that there's not now." Children were taught deference and respect. "No kids were allowed around when adults were talking." "We were all trying to help the older people." "They were quite a nice bunch, you never heard any swearing." "Being Portuguese, there was not much drinking in the family." Church services were obligatory on Sundays. "The priest either came to Reid or we went to Kuper." Every once in a while there would be a shopping trip to Mouat's store in the market town of Ganges on Salt Spring Island, where the Silveys were allowed to charge their goods if they didn't have the cash. "We would go by boat to Fernwood on the east side of Salt Spring and a friend would take us to the store in a horse and buggy."

Through the hard years, there were plenty of sociable times as well. "We used to go on picnics and make everything on the beach—we would take flour, baking powder,

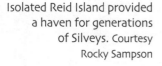

Isolated Reid Island provided a haven for generations of Silveys. Courtesy Rocky Sampson

The Silveys shopped at Mouat's store on Salt Spring Island, where they could get credit when they were short on cash.
Salt Spring Archives

etc.—we would catch the fish." Dances were held on weekends. Domingo and Tony both "played the button accordion" and Tony also "played the violin, guitar, mouth organ and Jew's harp." As for young Irene, "I got a kerchief and learned a dance, each person held an end of a kerchief, I put it around and over the head, we did this Portu-guese dance."

Traditional protocols held. "We had our brothers as chaperones at dances. We couldn't sit together and hold hands, we were told if we held hands or looked at each other we'd get pregnant." Another of Portuguese Joe's granddaughters recalled: "Mother said babies are under cabbage leaves, it was my older sister who had to tell us things." The prohibitions served their purpose. "For a large family, no one came home pregnant and no boys made girls pregnant."

Portuguese Joe's grandchildren and great-grandchildren were brought up by example, very much as their parents had been. "My aunt would say, 'get up, Irene, & watch me.'" "They taught the boys very well to log, fish, hunt, repair boats." The women "taught the young children cooking, bread making, canning, knitting, sew-ing, they took time out for us." Domingo's daughters Laura and Gloria recalled how "we learned how to cook, to make bread, to iron clothes." It was not just the girls who acquired such skills. Even "the men can cook whole meals." "We were taught how to wash clothes, we learned how to chop kindling, haul water, wash dishes, we all had something to do." The "men made their own bacon and ham," and this skill was also passed down. "We were taught very young how to accomplish every job, we had to do it over and over again until we got it."

When neither the residential school on Kuper Island nor the "white school" on Galiano would accept children of mixed race, the Silveys started up their own school on Reid Island, welcoming other families who found themselves in a similar bind.
Courtesy Art More and Laurie Williams

Some of the students at Silvey School commuted to school by boat.
Courtesy Art More and Laurie Williams

For all the lessons that were learned at home, formal schooling was also an essential part of all children's lives by this time, wherever they might live in British Columbia. Schooling became a family affair during the interwar years. Tony's two eldest children followed their mother to the Kuper Island residential school, but then the family was told that "it was not accepting half-breeds any more." Students "had to be full-blood Indians." This recollection coming down through the family is consistent with the general policy of the Department of Indian Affairs whereby only persons with status, which descended paternally and thereby excluded Tony's children, were permitted to live on reserves or attend residential school.

The nearest public school was on north Galiano. It was a log structure, which, according to family recollections, Domingo helped to build. Some of his older children attended, but "half the time we could not get to school on Galiano for bad weather." Not only that, increasingly "the white people didn't want us there, they said, 'we don't want you.'" One of Portuguese Joe's granddaughters explained that the children "weren't allowed to go to the white school." She summed up the dilemma in which the Silvey clan found themselves: "The Indians wouldn't accept us and neither would the whites. We might as well put it the way it was."

Like other British Columbia families in similar circumstances, the Silveys took matters into their own hands. On Gabriola Island, Josephine Silvey's brother Abe Crocker wangled a school near Silva Bay, where the extended family lived. On Reid Island the leadership came from Josephine's husband Domingo, their son Jack and his brother Tony. They named themselves school trustees and, in 1936, requested from the provincial Department of Education their own school on the island. More than 700 small rural elementary schools dotted the province, so officials in Victoria probably did not think twice about adding one more, or even about its name—Silvey School. At first, classes were held in the net shed located by the Mud Bay dike. When the shed became too dilapidated, the parents constructed a proper school.

"The parents got together and built the school and imported a couple of half-breed families to get enough children—the Crockers and the Rices." Domingo's wife Josephine was a Crocker, and the school-age members of her extended family lived during the school year in Portuguese Joe's old house, which was vacant after Lucy's death in 1934. "The Rices lived on their own island, Norway Island. When school started, nine of them had to paddle across. Then the Silveys built them a house across on the southern side of Reid Island." The Rice family originated with an American from Port Townsend in Washington and an Indian woman from Galiano Island. It was their son Charles's widow, a local Native woman, who took the initiative to ensure that their children were educated. To these were added Domingo's youngest child Gloria and the children of his son Jack and brother Tony. Tony's daughter Irene recalled with pride how, at the start of each year, "my father would buy us new pencils—we could choose our colours."

The published annual reports of the Department of Education indicate that Silvey School enrolled 15 to 18 children, mostly in the lower grades. The teacher's salary of $780 came primarily from the provincial government, with the "school district," in effect the parents, contributing another $20 to $100 a year to keep Silvey School in operation. It was not always possible to do so, because of falling average daily attendance. At least twice Silvey School was closed partway through the year.

Each year up to 18 children attended the one-room Silvey School at Mud Bay. Courtesy Art More and Laurie Williams

Portuguese Joe's son John with his sister Laura Silvey Thompson and his wife Laura McFadden Silvey behind him.
Courtesy Chris Thompson

The confirmation of Jack and Laura Silvey's daughters Patricia, Silvia, Della, Bernice and Eunice (dressed in white from left to right), on May 20, 1944, was a cause for celebration.

Learning was not necessarily an easy matter for these island children. "These were tough lessons—we would help each other." One of Tony's sons limped, "so we would pack his books." The self-selected trustees did the best they could, Tony's daughter Irene recalled. "At the school if any child was bad, trustees would take the child out and have a good talk to them and get them on the right track again. They always had time for the kids."

Tony's children moved most easily of their generation between their Portuguese and aboriginal inheritances. As Irene explained, "We had the best of two cultures." As well as living on Reid, "we were also raised with our adopted grandmother on Kuper." Irene had "lots of fun" as a child on Kuper. "We would go in a canoe and everyone got a paddle according to their size." Multilingualism continued to prevail, for her "adopted grandparents on Kuper Island always spoke Indian to us."

Whatever else Tony might do to make a living for his family, he remained a fisherman. "Fishing was his life, and he always returned to the industry after his excursions into other fields." He made his own spoons and lead lines when cod fishing or trolling on his boat, the *Last Chance*. As well as supporting his family, Tony took on the food fishery for Kuper Island from his father. Tony's three sons, who lived in the Ladysmith and Saltair districts, followed him into fishing. One of them took over the Penelakut food fishery.

Domingo Silvey, the patriarch of Reid Island, died in 1941. When he became seriously ill and could no longer support his family, the story in the family goes, everyone lent a hand. "Aunt Josie would go into town and, when the men would shake hands with her when she got off the boat, each one would give her $5 to go shopping. There was no welfare in those days." In death as in life, Portuguese Joe's oldest son successfully maintained the heritage his father held so dear. He was described on his death registration as "Portuguese" by racial origin.

Students at the Silvey School in June, 1937. Back row: Henry Crocker, Irene and Stan Silvey, Francis Crocker, Bernice Silvey and Joe Rice. Front row: Mary Crocker, Della Silvey, Rice child, Sylvia Silvey, Helen Rice, Gloria Silvey, Annie and Alex Rice, Ray, Jackie and Leonard Silvey. *Courtesy Art More and Laurie Williams*

Domingo's widow Josephine coped with his death by spending the summers at Steveston on the Fraser River or at one of the other coastal canneries. "She made a living making and mending nets. There were about five Indian ladies and mother mending nets." Her daughters sometimes went with her, for there was good money to be made. "$250 to make a net, $2.75 an hour to mend, you had to make a net in 10 hours or less." Josephine died in 1945.

Portuguese Joe's son Tony, who never owned any of the island, moved to nearby Ladysmith in about 1965 and died two years later. On his death certificate his daughter Edith recorded her bicultural family. She identified her paternal grandmother as Lucy Kwatleematt, thereby acknowledging Native descent, and her father as Portuguese.

After Domingo's death, Reid Island was divided among his children, and the entire island was eventually sold off—Domingo's eldest son Joe sold the last of it in 1974. Today there are about 30 holdings, most of them belonging to "summer people." Only the family cemetery, containing several generations of Silveys, gives a reminder of the important role Reid Island played for this coastal family.

Sylvia, Sanford, Darlene, Sam and John Silvey on a family outing in Pendrell Sound, north of Powell River. *Courtesy Eunice Weatherell*

Sons Away from Reid Island

Other Silvey children left Reid Island to embark on their own adventures. Portuguese Joe's second son Joseph, born in 1879, initiated a migration to Egmont, at the mouth of Jervis Inlet on the northeast edge of the Sechelt Peninsula. Some members of the Silvey family still live in the area: "Uncle Joe went in and found it a nice place and decided to settle there." According to Betty Keller and Rosella Leslie's history of the area, it was Portuguese Joe who first came across the spot. "Sometime during the late 1880s, he spent several years living in one of the bays near Egmont Point and fishing in Jervis Inlet."

Young Joe, together with his wife Maria King and two children, purchased 40 acres on the water at Egmont in 1904. Joe owned his own boat, and he seined, trolled and fished for lingcod. Five more children were born before Maria died in 1919. In the family tradition Joe mentored his sons into fishing. Over the next decade three of his children died in young adulthood, two from tuberculosis and the third by drowning after being swept overboard from a gillnetter. According to his grandson Leonard, the deaths devastated Joe. "I would sit with him for hours and he wouldn't say a word, he would just whittle and carve all these little boats. It was like he had died inside." At the time of his death in early 1940, Joe was living in Egmont. As with his older brother Domingo, his racial origin was shown on his death certificate as Portuguese. The identity was so entrenched that his son Ernie claimed both of Joe's parents—Portuguese Joe and Lucy—had been born in Portugal.

Portuguese Joe's second son Joseph initiated a small family migration to the village of Egmont near the mouth of the Sechelt Inlet.

Like his father before him, "Young Joe" took to the sea and taught his own sons how to fish. Courtesy Jessica Casey

Above: Frank Silvey (young Joe's son), Alfie Jeffries, Tom Wright, Harry Baines and young Joe Silvey.
Courtesy Jessica Casey

Opposite top: In keeping with tradition, Portuguese Joe's youngest son Henry became a fisherman who proudly named his boat the *Silvey*.
Courtesy Jessica Casey

Opposite bottom: Henry Silvey's wife Amelia Andrew.
Courtesy Jessica Casey

The two youngest Silvey sons, Manuel, born in 1886, and Henry, born in 1890, became fishermen almost as a matter of course. They took such pride in their work as a family endeavour that Henry named his boat the *Silvey*. His sometime partner in trawling and seining was Nick Stevens, a Salt Spring Islander linked by family and proximity. Nick's mother was the older sister of Maria King, married to Henry's brother Joe. Nick recalled that at the end of the season Henry Silvey "went to North Vancouver to visit." The reason he did so was decidedly romantic. Both Henry and his brother Manuel married sisters from North Vancouver. Charlotte and Amelia were the daughters of a Chilean man, who, according to family tradition, jumped ship at Vancouver in the early 1880s, when he was just 17.

Afraid of being caught, Balinto Fidele Sanhueza sought refuge from Chief Squamish Jim of the Mission Reserve in North Vancouver. He was soon living on a small farm with the chief's daughter, Kwaxtelut or Katherine. Charlotte was only four and Amelia Henriette just six months old when their mother died in 1890, at the age of 20. Sanhueza, who restyled himself Manuel Andrew, took as his new wife a local woman named Cecilia, who already had two children, including a daughter named Madeleine or Maggie, and who would herself die in 1909. One of the consequences of this upheaval was that all three girls—Charlotte, Amelia and Maggie—were sent to the Catholic residential school located on the Mission Reserve. On leaving school, Charlotte married a Chilean named Avaleno Savedra, by whom she had a son Frederick, born in February 1903.

Two years later Savedra was killed in a dynamite explosion while clearing land in North Vancouver, whereupon his widow married Manuel Silvey. Two years later, Charlotte's younger sister Amelia wed Manuel's younger brother Henry.

By virtue of marrying the Andrew sisters, Manuel and Henry Silvey acquired a large extended family. Manuel Andrew, who lived until 1945, encouraged visits to North Vancouver. His great-granddaughter Grace recalled the exhilarating experience, when she was a child, of walking across the newly opened Lion's Gate Bridge and then "up this huge hill" to reach his house. Charlotte and Amelia's maternal aunt had in 1894 married Willie Baker, son of the Silvey family's long-ago neighbour at Brockton Point. Charlotte's son Frederick Savedra had a family by the granddaughter of a Hawaiian, George Kamano, who was long settled on Harbledown Island off of northern Vancouver Island with his wife Claheara, or Pauline, from Fort Rupert. Charlotte and Amelia's stepsister Maggie lived at Chemainus with a Mexican known as Joe Rae, or Joshua Renosha. Grace remembered going there on the family fish boat and having Joe "teaching me Spanish, I was eight or nine, Grandmother said, 'Where did you learn those words?'...they were all swear words, and that was the end of my Spanish."

In about 1920, Henry and his family followed his older brother Joe from Reid Island to Egmont. The impetus was Henry's great discontent over Domingo's handling of Reid Island, their father's legacy. "I can see his boat piled high with stuff, he went to Jervis Inlet, and did not come back for three years." Henry skippered vessels for BC Packers, which operated canneries along the coast, and also seined, trolled and fished for cod with his own boat, the *Rose Silvey*. He had a saltery at Egmont, much like those operating on Reid and Galiano islands.

As always, the hard work was mixed with pleasure. Dances were held in the schoolhouse, and Henry sometimes played the guitar. These events gave Egmont's youthful enthusiasts an opportunity to dream. "When the floor manager said, 'Allemande left,' I would allemande left until he blew the whistle. I would then dance with the person I was facing. I tried my best to get close to the person I really liked." Henry and Amelia had six children and almost 60 years together before she died in 1966. He followed her two weeks later—dying of a broken heart, according to family legend.

Mano, as he was sometimes known within the family, was a "tugboat skipper who had his own boat and towed booms." Manuel and Charlotte had five children before he was drowned

One of the Silvey boats, the *Argent* heading up Jervis Inlet.
Courtesy Eunice Weatherell

in 1916 at Brockton Point, when his launch full of fish was run down by a tugboat. On board was his sister Mary's eldest son, who also perished. Charlotte Silvey was a housekeeper living at 786 East Hastings in Vancouver when she died on July 6, 1943. Her death certificate stated that she had been in the occupation for 35 years, or since her husband was killed. Her son proudly described her as Chilean by racial origin.

Both Manuel's and Henry's families preferred their Portuguese and Chilean identities over their aboriginality. Their neighbour Florence West, who moved to Egmont as a child, had no doubts that the families were, as she put it, "of Portuguese and Indian descent." Amelia in particular had good reason to downplay her family's aboriginal heritage. She used to tell about how, on being sent to residential school at age five, she had a needle pushed through her tongue for not being able to speak English.

She knew first-hand the racism that prevailed across mainstream British Columbia toward persons perceived as Indians or "half-breeds," and did not want her children and grandchildren to suffer its consequences.

Amelia would tell her children, "You can't be Native!" She emphasized to them: "We Silveys were only Portuguese, Chilean and a little bit of Greek from Maria King." A granddaughter reflected: "My grandmother was determined to protect us as well as she could. She was taking care of us in her own way. As long as Amelia was alive, we could not be Indian." Physical appearance counted. Charlotte in particular was remembered as "Hispanic."

The strategy of subordinating aboriginal to Portuguese identity did not always have the desired end. Manuel's son Tony, who lost his father in 1916 when he was only seven years old, lost touch with his Portuguese heritage. His daughter identified him solely as a "Native Indian" on his death in 1972.

Lucy's Daughters

Portuguese Joe and Lucy's two daughters, Mary and Lena, divided their loyalties between the men in their lives. Initially Mary followed the marital path taken by her older half-sisters, but although she did her best to sustain her children, she could not always manage the feat. Her married daughter Laura Roberts was living with her in Vancouver when, at age 21, she fell out of a window and died of a fractured skull. In the same year, 1914, Mary's eldest daughter from her second marriage, Mina, married into the Wilson family, the same Fraser River fishing clan that her cousin Joe would shortly join.

Joe and Lucy's daughter Mary (left) was a very talented basket weaver. Beside her is Laura G. Silvey.
Courtesy Eunice Weatherell

Portuguese Joe's youngest daughter Lena was a rebel, whose great love for her family did not stop her from living an unconventional life.
Courtesy Chris Thompson

Over time, Mary turned more and more to her birth family. She lived on her brother Henry's property at Egmont and then got her own place nearby. Their neighbour Florence West recalled Mary and her then husband Harry Buss as "colourful characters." Mary had what might be termed personality. "She used to cause a lot of trouble with her gossiping but if anyone got sick she would be the first to help. She lived in Egmont and she raised her grandson Arthur."

In 1936 Vancouver celebrated the 50th anniversary of its incorporation, and the city encouraged early residents to participate in Jubilee events. Mary was determined to do so, which speaks to her toughness of character and also to her integration of her paternal and maternal inheritances. Wanting to ensure that her father's contribution to city building was acknowledged, she paid a visit to the Vancouver archivist, Major Matthews. He did not know quite what to make of Joe Silvey's daughter. "She has come to Vancouver to witness the Golden Jubilee festivities of her native home, but has come without money, and is trying to sell Indian basketry, of her own make, to raise the small sum sufficient for her humble needs." Mary was, by Matthews's description, "a stout woman with the characteristics of an Indian, and in this respect takes after her mother, who was a full-blooded Sechelt Indian, she cannot read or write, but is very clever in making Indian basketry." Mary was by then becoming somewhat hazy about the events in her life and died in1941 at Essondale Mental Hospital near Vancouver. Her husband gave the information and described her, unlike any of the other Silvey children, as an "Indian."

The youngest Silvey was Lena. She was just six when her father died and, perhaps for that reason, was much more her own person than his other daughters. According to her nieces, "Lena was a free spirit." Her mother was repeatedly frustrated by Lena's antics. She lived for a time in Chemainus, where Lucy's partner Joe Watson worked as a longshoreman, and when she came home would "la-di-dah." Sometimes she had a man in tow. "Aunt Lena was always introducing her new husband, 'This is your new uncle, my dear.'"

Lena's resourcefulness in life made her the one her brothers leaned on when something went wrong. When Domingo built his son Jack his first fishing boat in 1918, he named it *Lena* after his youngest sister. "It was Lena who they used for advice. They called her in when there was a problem in the family. Auntie Lena was like a matriarch on Reid Island." Lena, her five children and an American husband lived for a time near the saltery in the Silvey compound at Egmont. Then she bought property and built a house of her own. Lena's husband went off to the Second World War and, the story goes, "when he came back she had another man there." Lena was described as a widow on her death in 1957.

Portuguese Joe's Legacy

Portuguese Joe Silvey was a determined, resourceful, hardworking man who left an important trace on British Columbia. He was one of the earliest entrepreneurs in today's Vancouver. He contributed in diverse and significant ways to the development of the province's fishing industry. He understood the importance of community to family survival in difficult times, and he laid the foundation for a largely self-sustaining way of life.

The Silvey legacy is considerable. Portuguese Joe had six sons and four daughters who survived into adulthood. Through their marriages, they consolidated a hybrid coastal society that originated with the gold rush and continues to contribute to the making of British Columbia. At least 70 grandchildren were born, well over half of them bearing the Silvey surname, and many more great-grandchildren, and so on into the present day.

Portuguese Joe inculcated into his children the traditional Portuguese values of his childhood, and these they sought to pass down to the next generation. Sometimes the values have transferred at a personal cost, such as what transpired when Henry and Amelia's daughter Violet became pregnant at age 16 at Christmas 1927, by her cousin Ernie, son of Joseph and Maria. Violet was promptly married off to a much older man who had been a friend of her grandfather, Portuguese Joe. However much in love the young couple might be, Portuguese tradition dictated that cousins did not wed. "Her father was very old-fashioned and Portuguese—that was a no-no, they were cousins." Violet was not to be deterred. She ran off on her wedding night to her Aunt Lena, then living in Vancouver. There she stayed until her daughter Grace was born the next August, in the hospital after which she was named. Violet then took off alone, up the coast in search of her beloved Ernie, who was out fishing for the season. For a time it seemed that the only option was to have baby Grace adopted out—that is, until Aunt Lena stepped in and persuaded her sister-in-law Amelia to come and get the infant.

Grace was raised mostly at Egmont by her grandparents, Henry and Amelia, and she found herself subject to much the same restrictions as her mother had been.

Henry and Amelia Silvey's children Bill, Violet and Ky.
Courtesy Jessica Casey

Amelia Silvey with her
daughter Rose and
granddaughter Grace.
Courtesy Jessica Casey

She recalled being carefully chaperoned to dances and on other social occasions. "Portuguese descent, you're old fashioned, you know. You were chaperoned all the time." Grace's solace came from her beloved Aunt Lena. Now living at Egmont, Lena taught embroidery and fancywork to the niece she had rescued from adoption. Like her mother, Grace was pushed in traditional Portuguese style toward an arranged marriage, to a man who fished with her father. But before the actual wedding, she was able to escape to her biological parents, who were by now settled with a family.

The Silveys' strong sense of Portuguese identity was reinforced by countrymen living nearby and also by visits from relatives. Portuguese Joe's oldest daughter Elizabeth used to receive letters from "cousins in Massachusetts," whom she recalled as children of her father's sister. Portuguese Joe's nephew "came twice to see them at Reid Island to make certain his uncle was receiving merchandise sent from the family at New Bedford, Massachusetts, USA." Tony's daughter Irene described how, in about 1945, "a cousin in the states that had a vineyard, a big vineyard in California, came to see dad in a yellow Cadillac." Antonio Christian de Silvia got as far as Ladysmith, but could not find the family because he was looking for them by his own surname. Eventually the "fisheries officer came and told Pa that somebody was looking for him in Ladysmith." Irene and her siblings were taken to meet him. "Out of respect we called him uncle, but he was a first cousin." The children were sent back home to Reid Island, while their father Tony stayed on to visit with this new-found relative who "took over the Europe Hotel and stayed a week there."

However much family members might conceive of themselves as Portuguese, they had to negotiate their aboriginality and, even more, their hybridity. All her life, Portuguese Joe's eldest daughter Elizabeth valued the understandings her mother Khaltinaht had given her about her Squamish and Musqueam ancestry. For her younger half-brother Tony, it was his wife Alice Aleck who played that role. Other Silvey children and grandchildren were ambivalent about their maternal inheritance, and they had pragmatic reasons for these feelings. Domingo's eldest son Joe considered World War I an important learning experience in terms of his racial inheritance. He trained in England, which was a revelation: "The British saw us as soldiers, they treated us as soldiers." The sense of equality Joe experienced there was in sharp distinction to Canada, where he was scorned and treated as an inferior.

For a long time in British Columbia, almost no one who had a choice wanted to be an Indian or a "half-breed." As Tony's daughter Irene recalled, "Auntie Josie [Domingo's wife] and Grandma [Silvey] and Grandma on Kuper would send the children out and speak Indian to each other, they didn't want the children to know that they spoke Indian." Asked when the racism stopped, a granddaughter responded, "maybe it stopped in the late '40s or '50s," and, on reflection, "no, it isn't really stopped." Referring to a Silvey grandson, a Chemainus businessman claimed in the 1970s that "the

Domingo and Josephine Silvey's son Jack.
Courtesy Art More and Laurie Williams

The "Reid Island Beauties"
(Laura, Pat, Della, Sylvia and
Eunice) going for a dip at
Starvation Bay, Valdes Island.
Courtesy Chris Thompson

old Indian owes me money." Descendants were caught. Outsiders equated the Silvey family's near-subsistence lifestyle with their stereotypical perceptions of aboriginal ways. Whatever the measure, "everyone wanted to be white people," to quote Irene, but the Silveys were not.

In the second generation and to a considerable extent subsequently, the Silveys coped by relying on each other and marrying within familiar settings. They were resourceful and strategic. As descendant after descendant has explained, "it seems like everyone knows everyone else among the old families." The water linked coastal and island families. Their children, particularly those who had aboriginal mothers, were given every encouragement to intermarry, and all six of Portuguese Joe's sons and his eldest daughter did so. Proximity of and adherence to Catholicism encouraged relationships, but so did the racial antipathies of the day. "Families of mixed race stuck together, they had to." Joe Silvey's other three daughters looked to newcomer men, who turned to mixed-heritage women when newcomer females were in short supply. Whether or not the tensions inherent in such situations played a role, none of Portuguese Joe's daughters had relationships as outwardly stable as those of their brothers.

Some descendants, by choice or circumstance, came to see themselves over time as principally Native, others as primarily Portuguese. "There's a definite divide in the

family between Portuguese and Indian Silveys." Due to the demographic imbalance and the expectation that a woman would in any case adopt her husband's identity, descendants through the female line have found it easier to shed their aboriginality, should they so choose. It is only in the present generation that negative attitudes toward aboriginality and mixed race have moderated in the larger society. Family members now take pride in reclaiming their Native heritage, as Joe's oldest daughter Elizabeth attempted to do with middling success in her last years.

The self-confidence that families like the Silveys could realize by working in the resource sector has been a powerful counterpoint to issues of racial identity. Economic survival was never easy—it required hard physical labour to make a living. The Silveys have made that commitment for a century and a half in British Columbia. Portuguese Joe's granddaughter Irene has characterized the Silveys as "seine boat skippers, cod fishermen, so many things, they could do anything to do with logging and fishing." Their way of life gave them self-confidence and a strong sense of self. "If there was no sea and no fishing, there would be no me," as Portuguese Joe's great-grandson Leonard put it.

A newspaper obituary of young Joe and Maria's son Frank, born in Chemainus in 1901, says that with his wife Violet at his side, "he died last month as he had lived, fishing the Strait of Georgia waters from which he had wrested a living over the past six decades." This description from 1972 applies to any number of Portuguese Joe's descendants: "Silvey was skipper of a seine boat at the age of 16 and spent many years trolling, packing, longlining, gillnetting, and cod fishing…The industry veteran began fishing with his father as a boy and was skipping a seiner before he was out of his teens. During his long career, he worked in virtually all sections of the industry, as a seiner, troller, longliner, tenderman, gillnetter and cod fisherman." The strength that marked Silvey women as well as men is evident in the story, for it was Violet who on her own "brought their 31-foot *Francis Point* back to Deep Bay." In the space for "racial origin" on Frank Silvey's death certificate, his son proudly put down "Portuguese."

The ethos of hard work that has guided and sustained the Silvey family from the time of Portuguese Joe into the present day is captured in the lines of a poem written by his great-great-granddaughter Jessica Silvey Casey, in honour of her father:

A fisherman
Is all I will ever be
I was born to a family
That lived to sail the sea.
The tides of change
May flow
In and out
But this
I will never doubt
Wherever there are salmon
I will surely go
It is the only way
Of life
I know.

Or, to put the matter another way, "I will not forget who I am, here I am, I'm a Silvey, and I'm proud of it."

Opposite top: Ken Silvey near Domingo's old home.
Courtesy Eunice Weatherell

Opposite bottom: Della Silvey, Domingo's first grandchild born with the Silvey name.
Courtesy Eunice Weatherell

Below left: Jack Silvey's packer *Great Northern 9*.
Courtesy Eunice Weatherell

Afterword

by Rocky Sampson, great-great-grandson of Portuguese Joe Silvey

What a delight it was to read *The Remarkable Adventures of Portuguese Joe Silvey*. Dr. Barman, I was very impressed by the way in which you handled the large and overwhelming family I call mine. I find there are so many named Josephine, Joseph, Amelia and many other names that can be confusing, but you kept the right person and the right "Joe" in line. Your book is my book, is our book, and this book shows that in a world where strangers come and go it is great to have a sense of belonging and family. Family is not always perfect by any means but it is all we have at the end of the day. We overcome challenges and obstacles with family. We pull together in good times and sad, with family. We forgive as family and we love as family.

I remember as a boy when I first went to my mom's home, "Reid Island." I was still a small child and my Great Uncle Joe and Aunt Amelia picked us up at Chemainus in his small wooden green boat. The boat was so tiny I thought we would sink, but it took me, my two brothers, parents and Uncle Joe and Aunt Amelia the distance to Reid Island. The journey was magical as we slowly motored our way through the islands, tides and sun. Time stood still and time did not matter. I recall coming ashore at Reid Island and setting foot on land that was somehow familiar. The dry grasses of summer, the scent of arbutus leaves and sea air were all familiar to my soul. Reid Island was a special place for us kids to explore. "Qulus," Reid Island's Hul'qumi'num name, means "quiet and peaceful place" and I think it lives up to its real name. We had grown up on islands but I felt a connection to Reid. I can recall finding a lizard in the cemetery by the sea; I followed his whipping tail to his hiding place in the middle of the cemetery. Then I realized where I was. I stood in silence listening to the tide in the channel and the waves splash on the rocks . . . the magic was simply knowing I was part of all around me, part of family.

On that same first trip I recall nightfall too. It must have been the first night on our visit as the coal oil lamps were out and candles burned to make light for family stories. I recall all went fine until great Uncle Joe began telling family ghost stories. Suddenly my hair stood on end and fear filled me. My fears took me away and I was scared beyond belief! But the trip was far too short and far too soon we were heading home.

What strikes my memory most was the trunk Uncle Joe had, filled with family memorabilia and photographs, some yellow with age and others printed on tin. I recall placing it all together: the pictures, ghost stories, the smell of the sea, the smell of the wild grasses in the cemetery and the feeling of family and love. Reid Island wasn't my home Island but it was my connection to my people.

They say we don't remember days but rather we recall moments in our lives; I tend to think we recall it all. When I go to Reid Island today I taste the apples, grapes and berries, I smell the honeysuckle wild roses and mosses. I smell the blackened earth, dry like summer. I hear the distant rip of tide at Porlier Pass. My hands feel the sun-baked sandstone. I see how the sun glints a million sparkles on the sea, I remember it all, not just a moment.

Sources

Portuguese Joe Silvey's story was written at the request of his great-great-great-grandsons, Kyle and Cole Silvey. They and their teacher Pauline Falck at Quadra Elementary School at Quathiaski Cove, British Columbia, heard me talk about Portuguese Joe on Mark Forsythe's show *Almanac* on CBC Radio in the fall of 1998. They wanted to know more about this man who shared their surname and who, they speculated, might be related to them. I took "The Remarkable Adventures," written for them, to a Silvey family reunion at Ladysmith the following spring. Since then, numerous copies have been shared with descendants and others. Manuel Azevedo, a historian of the Portuguese community in British Columbia who is from Pico Island in the Azores, as was Joe Silvey, introduced the story to the Portuguese community in Vancouver and Toronto.

Many persons have added their voices to this expanded text. Among those sharing memories, photographs or other materials are Marilyn Baines, Gloria Blomley, Barrie Bradshaw, Jessica Casey, Mackie Chase, Margaret Hall Corbett, Gordon de Frane, Florence West Dubois, Grace Faulds, Marie Gabara, Irene Griffith, Brenda Hammond, Maria Lima, Marie Malbon, Jane Marston, Art More, Rose Peddie, Phyllis Roberts, Sylvia Sampson, Leonard Silvey, Rose Silvey, Marlene Smith, Chris Thompson, Laura Thompson and Eunice Weatherell. I owe a special thank you to Rocky Sampson for his contributions to the book. I am grateful to Howard White for suggesting Portuguese Joe's story merited publication, and to Shyla Seller, Mary Schendlinger, Vici Johnstone, and Alicia Miller for guiding it there. I have received much useful advice as to what I got wrong and what is right. Sometimes I have had to make choices as to which sources appear most reliable and consistent with other information. I take full responsibility for any misunderstandings and errors that may have resulted. Joe Silvey's story is just that, a story.

The most vivid stories about Portuguese Joe come from his eldest daughter Elizabeth, who shared her memories with Major J.S. Matthews, Vancouver City Archivist. The two had more than a dozen conversations between October 1938 and October 1943, about a year and a half before her death. Matthews would type up his notes, either as they were talking or afterwards. He would read the text back to her for any changes or additions, and she would then sign the transcript with a shaky hand. It is important to keep in mind that Elizabeth's stories are only her recollections and some parts of them may have become exaggerated over time. On the other hand, they remained remarkably consistent over the five years she talked with Major Matthews.

I have also drawn from Major Matthews's conversations and correspondence with Thomas Bryant, Alice Crakanthorp, Thomas Fisher, Jim Franks, W.A. Grafton, Christine Thomas Jack, Jennie Beale Jeffries (in Silvey file), Tom MacInnes, William Mackie, Mr. and Mrs. Joseph Silvey, Calvert Simson, Charles Tate and Madeline Williams (widow of John "Gassy Jack" Deighton). Elizabeth Silvey's sister Mary Buss talked with Major Matthews twice in June 1936. Transcripts of all his conversations and related materials are in City of Vancouver Archives [CVA], Add. Ms. 54, excepting Bryant, which is in Matthews, *Early Vancouver*, Vol. 4, typescript CVA, Add. Ms. 97. Leo and Gaylia Nelson talked about the Silva family on March 7, 1975. The transcript is held in the British Columbia Archives [BCA], Ms. 242.

Just as with each of our stories, some parts of Portuguese Joe's remarkable adventures are easier to disentangle than others. Silvey family photos, correspondence and other papers going back in time a century and more were kept on Reid Island following its sale out of the family and, sadly, lost in a house fire there in 1978.

Basic information we take for granted about ourselves sometimes remains a bit of a mystery. Because Joseph Silvey could not do so, others wrote his name for him. When necessary, he wrote an X to confirm the accuracy of what he "signed" his name to. Among spellings put down on paper were Silva, Silvey, Silvia, Silver and Silvia Seamens. At his marriage, he described himself to the Catholic priest who performed the ceremony as Joseph Silvy, born in about 1834 to John Silvy and Francesca Hyacintha on Piopiko Island, Portugal. Brenda Hammond and Manuel Azevedo have separately initiated searches through records of Catholic baptisms on Pico Island. The single plausible record names the parents as João Joze, or John Joseph, de Simas and Francisca Jacinta, not that different from the names Joe used. Their son José, or Joseph, was born on April 23, 1828, six years before the birth year Portuguese Joe gave for himself. It is very likely but not certain that they were the same person.

Written sources include vital statistics kept by churches and the provincial government, preemption records, wills and probates, and the manuscript censuses for 1881, 1891 and 1901, all in BCA, excepting St. Ann's baptisms and marriages, held at St. Edward's Church, Duncan. Other information can be found in Robert James Roberts, Diary, BCA, A/E/R54/R54A; Kuper Island Indian Industrial School records, BCA, Ms. 1267; "Chief Squamish Jim, Sikemain, 1850–1924," CVA, Add. Ms. 5; Crown Lands records, BCA, GR 1088, box 1, files 1, 33; Soldiers of the First World War, National Archives of Canada web site; Joseph Domingo Silvey, "The Silvey Family," in Lillian Gustafson, comp., *Memories of the Chemainus Valley: A History of People* (Victoria: Chemainus Valley Historical Society, 1978); Florence Dubois, *William Jeffries and Other Pioneers of the Sunshine Coast* (privately published, 1996); Florence Tickner, *Fish Hooks & Caulk Boots, Raincoast Chronicles 14* (Madeira Park: Harbour, 1992); and Betty C. Keller and Rosella M. Leslie, *Bright Seas, Pioneer Spirits: The Sunshine Coast* (Victoria: Horsdal & Schubart, 1996).

I have also drawn from general sources. The Azores are introduced in Jerry Williams, *And Yet They Come: Portuguese Immigration from the Azores to the United States* (New York: Center for Migration Studies, 1982); whaling and its relationship to the Azores in Elmo P. Hohman, *The American Whaleman: A Study of Life and Labor in the Whaling Industry* (New York: Longmans, Green & Co., 1928); Briton Cooper Busch, *"Whaling Will Never Do for Me": The American Whaleman in the Nineteenth Century* (Lexington: University Press of Kentucky, 1994); and E. Davis, Robert E. Gallman, and Karin Gleiter, *In Pursuit of Leviathan: Technology, Institutions, Productivity, and Profits in American Whaling, 1816–1906* (Chicago: University of Chicago Press, 1997). Portuguese Joe's cabin at Point Roberts is described in R. Byron Johnson, *Very Far West Indeed: A Few Rough Experiences on the North-West Pacific Coast* (London: Sampson Low, Marston, Low, & Searle, 1872). Descriptions of Joe Silvey as a fisherman come from Major Matthews's sconversations noted above and also from Robert Brown, "The Land of the Hydahs, a spring journey north," in BCA, ms. 794, Vol. 2, file 10; and testimony of Joseph Mannion, in the appeal of Attorney General vs. Canadian Pacific Railway, Victoria, January 4, 1905, CVA. His activities in Gastown are described in Joseph Silvy to Chief Commissioner of Lands and Works, New Westminster, May 15, 1868; Joseph Silvy to A.T. Bushby, Burrard Inlet, December 15, 1870; A.T. Bushby to Colonial Secretary, Burrard Inlet, December 28, 1870; and E. Brown to A.T. Bushby, New Westminster, December 28, 1870, in BCA, GR1372, files F159a and F245. The activities of the British Columbia Reserve Commission are detailed in Department of Indian Affairs, RG10, Vol. 3645, file 7936, microfilm reel C-10113.

Information on William Bridge comes from John Rodger Burnes, *Saga of a Municipality In Its Formative Days 1891–1907* (North Vancouver: n.p., 1972?), and J.S. Matthews, *Early Vancouver*, Vol. 1 (Vancouver: City of Vancouver Archives, 1932), 160E. Navvy Jack Thomas is mentioned in William Scott, "The Early Story of North Vancouver," *Museum and Art Notes* (Art, Historical and Scientific Association of Vancouver), 2nd ser., Vol. 1, No. 2 (March 1950), 14; note with "Daughter of West Van Pioneer Dies," unidentified newspaper, March 25, 1960, CVA; and Charles W. Cates, *Tidal Action in British Columbia Waters* (North Vancouver: n.p., 1952). Nick Stevens recalled fishing with Henry Silvey in Nick Stevens, "Ice on the Fraser," 1949, typescript in Delta Archives, DE-48.

Newspaper stories quoted from are "Naturalized," *British Colonist*, March 25, 1867; "Gassy Jack," *Vancouver News*, September 14, 1886; Whyawhy, "Poor Jack's End," *Vancouver News*, September 15, 1886; Alan Morley, "Romance of Vancouver," *Sun*, May 21, 1940; "Portuguese Joe," *Province*, July 31, 1945; Nick Stevens, "Old Picture Stirs Memories," *Fisherman*, December 18, 1961; "Old Picture Prompts Story," *Fisherman*, January 19, 1962; "Death of Tony Silvey Snaps Link with Past," *Fisherman*, February 10, 1967; "Veteran Frank Silvey Stricken on Grounds," *Fisherman*, July 7, 1972; "Fisherman Passes Away," *Nanaimo Daily Free Press*, June 26, 1972; and Helen Plester, "History Comes Alive," *Daily Colonist*, June 26, 1977.

Index